D0880978

MEREDITH:
A CHANGE OF MASKS

Meredith: A Change of Masks

A Study of the Novels

by

GILLIAN BEER

UNIVERSITY OF LONDON

THE ATHLONE PRESS

1970

Published by
THE ATHLONE PRESS
UNIVERSITY OF LONDON
at 2 *Gower Street London* WC1

Distributed by Tiptree Book Services Ltd
Tiptree, Essex

Australia and New Zealand
Melbourne University Press

U.S.A.
Oxford University Press Inc
New York

0 485 11122 5

Printed in Great Britain by
WILLIAM CLOWES AND SONS, LIMITED
LONDON AND BECCLES

PREFACE

MEREDITH, like Clough, is a writer whom individuals discover with excitement for themselves. To say that you are writing on Meredith's novels, is often to find yourself engrossed in discussion and argument with people who were strangers a moment earlier. This stimulating contact with people frequently remote from the professional study of English literature has been one of the most constant sources of enjoyment that the work has brought me. I am particularly grateful to those friends and acquaintances who read Meredith in their youth earlier in this century, when his intellectual prestige was at its height, and who have offered me fresh and often trenchant insights into his significance for their generation.

I have had the pleasure of conversation with Meredith scholars such as Norman Kelvin, L. T. Hergenhan and Margaret Harris, and with graduate students from a number of universities. I am particularly grateful to Professor Phyllis Bartlett for her generosity in sharing her great knowledge of Meredith, to Professor Kathleen Tillotson for her encouragement and guidance, and to Professor Barbara Hardy for her valuable suggestions and criticisms. My pupils have constantly enlivened me by their enthusiasm for much else besides Meredith.

I owe a particular debt to the Curators of Yale University Library, the Widener Collection, Widener Library, the Berg Collection, New York Public Library and to the Pierpont Morgan Library, New York, for allowing me to examine and—where appropriate—quote from the unpublished material in their care; I must thank the staffs of these libraries for their kindness and efficiency. I am also grateful to the Librarians and staff of the British Museum; Senate House Library, University of London; the Libraries of Manchester and of Liverpool Universities, and the Cambridge University Library. I began this book while Andrew Bradley Fellow at Liverpool University and completed it as a Research Fellow, and, subsequently, Fellow of Girton College, Cambridge, to whose Mistress and Fellows I owe a continuing debt of gratitude.

I have contributed an essay on '*One of our Conquerors*: language and music' to a volume of new essays, edited by Ian Fletcher. This is to be published shortly and supplements the discussion of *One of our Conquerors* in the present study. Some of the material in Chapter 4 originally appeared in the *Review of English Studies* and *Nineteenth-Century Fiction* and an earlier version of Chapter 6 appeared in *A Review of English Literature*. I am grateful to the editors for permitting me to use the material here.

My greatest indebtedness is to my family. To my mother for her constant and sustained encouragement, to my children for their total unconsciousness of Meredith, and, most of all, to my husband for his never-failing insight and help.

Cambridge G.B.
April 1970

CONTENTS

'We live in what we have done—in the idea'

(Letter of 1884)

'Each life its critic deed reveals'

('Empedocles')

George Meredith

The rhetorician would deceive his neighbours,
The sentimentalist himself; while art
Is but a vision of reality.

('Ego Dominus Tuus')

W. B. Yeats

NOTE

All references to Meredith's published novels are to the Standard Edition, the pagination of which corresponds to that of the Memorial Edition.

Introduction

MEREDITH'S work has always aroused strong antipathy and admiration. From the first, hostile critics have seen him as merely obscure and pretentious. Yet his admirers in his own time greeted him as a writer whose intensity of insight and expressiveness made him something more than a literary figure—something closer to a prophetic consciousness. Leonard Woolf explained that Meredith attracted his own younger generation because he rejected 'the cosmic and social assumptions of Thackeray and Dickens . . . challenging their standards of morality'.[1]

Through his exploration of the possibilities of the novel as a form Meredith discovered new channels for consciousness to flow in. He was a consciously experimental writer; his technical innovations pushed the novel almost as far as it would go towards the compression and ellipsis of poetry. His work is not only interesting in itself but crucial to an understanding of the way the English novel developed towards the end of the nineteenth century. He was the first to express a major shift of sensibility, registered in the increasing introspection, lyricism, psychological analysis and symbolistic organisation of the novel in the ensuing period.

For any sympathetic modern reader of Meredith's novels antipathy and admiration are likely to alternate. Some of his views must now seem remote, even naive: his assurance that man is evolving towards perfection; his belief in the inevitably healing power of laughter; his assertion that mental and physical punishment brace a man. Yet the exploring intelligence which informs his writing should make us wary of dismissing what is alien as meaningless for us.

His novels never sacrifice insight to dogma: they work through a process of testing and scrutiny. The free play of his emotions and intelligence involves him in constant reappraisal. He is sensitive to the way a change of perspective can alter the nature of experience.

No novelist has ever been more conscious of the closeness to each other of comedy and tragedy. His nervous, even hectic, awareness of the other face of either experience leaves him only at rare moments of intense lyricism. In one of his late poems, 'The Two Masks', he describes the struggle between the Muses of Comedy and Tragedy.

Tragedy knows:

> that one museful ripple
> Along those lips of rose with tendril hooks
> Forebodes disturbance in the springs of pathos,
> Perchance may change of masks midway demand,
> Albeit the man rise mountainous as Athos,
> The woman wild as Cape Leucadia stand.

The Comic Muse fastens upon those who 'strive . . . to outleap our human features' and fail to obey 'Reason's ordinance'. Irony is unremitting in Meredith's work—but it is an irony which depends on strong primary emotion.

Part of the modern rejection of Meredith seems to me to be based on misreading—where it is not simply received opinion. He is commonly referred to as a precious writer, intent on his own wit. He *is* a witty writer and like Joyce, who felt a strong kinship with him, he is a part of that other tradition of the English novel which moves through Lyly and Sterne: dramatic plot is abandoned, ornamentation flourishes, and brilliance is an end in itself as well as an instrument of exploration. But Meredith's intensely experimental approach to the novel is always a part of his moral concern with human personality. By the method of fiction he makes many of the discoveries that Freud was making, but he uses them to reach absolute moral judgments: 'These are the ways egoism works and this is what is wrong with it', rather than 'These are the ways the ego has been observed to work'. Meredith tries to combine the roles of sage and explorer, bard and craftsman.

He is interested above all in the inner life of his characters and particularly in those levels which are beneath conscious control. The novel, as a form, is particularly appropriate to the exploration of the 'submerged self'.[2] The process of silent reading approximates to the life of thought and feeling rather than to speech and action; the novel becomes a prolonged, intermittent part of the reader's unspoken daily life. But Meredith is not simply a novelist of sensibility: he recognises that personality is most vividly focussed in action and that drama can be the most economical means of expressing what a character cannot acknowledge about himself. In his attempt to be faithful to his material he is forced to find new ways of relating plot and character. Equally, he tries to evolve a style capable of dramatising the characters' *unformulated* impulses and perceptions.

Henry James (writing of Meredith's letters) asserted that he lacked the aesthetic curiosity 'to be a true artist in fiction'.[3] Yet Meredith's late period preceded James's by some fifteen years and showed the possibilities of a narrative style based on an individual idiosyncratic sensibility rather than on common speech. James's response to Meredith has a mingled enthusiasm and acidity which is perhaps the result of unwillingly acknowledged kinship. His attack on Meredith in Edith Wharton's *A Backward Glance* reads like an attack on his own late style:

Words—words—poetic imagery, metaphors, epigrams, descriptive passages! How much did any of them weigh in the baggage of the authentic novelist? . . . Meredith, he continued, was a sentimental rhetorician, whose natural indolence or congenital insufficiency, or both, made him, in life as in his art, shirk every climax, dodge around it, and veil its absence in a fog of eloquence.[4]

I would suggest, on the contrary, that Meredith's rhetoric is a precise instrument. His aesthetic curiosity provides the energy for the writing and rewriting of his novels and is a part of his profound curiosity about the workings of character and action. He rewrote meticulously to achieve specific effects. The unpublished early drafts of the novels, as well as his working notebooks, show him progressing towards an ever more exact and intricate record of his characters. He himself wrote of 'My Dnd. Dnd. Dnd. uncertain workmanship' and the revisions show him struggling with the problem of 'when to dramatise and when to narrate' which he held to be 'the novelist's chief lesson' after the construction of plot.[5]

The manuscript notebooks and early drafts which I refer to and cite in this book provide additional evidence that Meredith is a novelist whose originality of insight into personality and into the possibilities of his craft amply rewards us for the intensity of reading he demands.[6] He is also—a more dangerous attraction for the critic—a novelist whose ambitious imperfection suggests more about the potentialities and limits of the novel-form than a fully achieved artist would do.

Recent criticism of Meredith has tended to be primarily concerned with biography and with the intellectual milieu of his work: Professor Lionel Stevenson's *The Ordeal of George Meredith* and Professor Norman Kelvin's *A Troubled Eden* show how much these approaches can contribute to our understanding of Meredith's work and I have found their books extremely helpful in formulating my own rather different critical approach. This study is focussed primarily on Meredith's art as a novelist. I have organised my case for a re-appraisal of his achievement through a concentrated study of six of the novels, although many of my illustrations are taken from the rest of his work. The six novels I have chosen demonstrate the range of his accomplishment; they all merit and repay close analysis. Moreover, each of them brings very consciously into focus artistic problems with which Meredith was preoccupied: for example, the handling of autobiographical material, in *The Ordeal of Richard Feverel*; the relationship between rhetoric and action, in *Beauchamp's Career*; the nature of realism, in *Diana of the Crossways*. Such topics are important to Meredith in all the novels but they become part of the argument in these particular works. For this reason I have discussed general topics, such as style, the narrator's role, and Meredith's handling of comic and tragic mode, chiefly in relationship to the novel most specifically concerned with them. The chapter headings indicate the organisation. I have used historical and textual material freely where this enlarges our understanding of Meredith's creativity.

Meredith's kinship of methods and perceptions often seems to be with twentieth-century writers rather than with his own earlier contemporaries. The fragmented chronology, the refracted experience, the dense flux of symbol and metaphor in his novels, all link him with later writers. Without refashioning him into a modern novelist, it may be possible for readers now to approach him more directly than at any time since the eighteen-nineties.

Professor C. L. Cline, writing of the rich tradition of biographical and historical scholarship in studies of Meredith, said in 1964: 'What has not been done extensively is to re-examine Meredith's novels in the light of contemporary standards of criticism. Only when this has been done can Meredith take his rightful place in the critical canon'.[7] I hope that the present study will go some way towards answering this need.

I

The Ordeal of Richard Feverel
Autobiography and Fiction

IN the course of his long creative life Meredith completed thirteen full-length novels: the first, *The Ordeal of Richard Feverel*, was published in 1859, in the same year as George Eliot's first full-length novel, *Adam Bede*. The last, *The Amazing Marriage*, appeared in 1895, alongside H. G. Wells's *The Time Machine*. The novels share certain insistent themes, the most pervasive of which is the power of unconscious egoism. In some ways Meredith's ideas seem extraordinarily set: observations and situations recur throughout his work. But they recur with the energy and inventiveness of obsession rather than with monolithic assurance. The manifestations of egoism are so devious that this one theme alone can include the whole variety of social being. And although many of Meredith's pre-occupations remain constant, the novels themselves are remarkably diverse. He usually rejects his last piece of work completely—and often seems to set out to write its opposite.

Meredith's first published fiction was *The Shaving of Shagpat*, which George Eliot reviewed enthusiastically: 'In exuberance of imagery, in picturesque wildness of incident, in significant humour, in aphoristic wisdom *The Shaving of Shagpat* is a new Arabian night'.[1] In this narrative fantasy Meredith was able to give play to his intensely imagistic perceptions. Imagery becomes both embellishment and substance; at the same time the book shows his capacity for story-telling. Several persisting themes emerge: growth through trials, the dangers of illusion, the saving power of humour—but all these are held within a form which calls on the Arabian exotic and also on the eighteenth-century rationalisation of the exotic. Meredith is writing a parody of Eastern tales but this does not detach him from his material so much as define its strangeness. The world he shows is absolute, exotic and harmless. It is a world of escape and dreams with no pressing relevance to human problems. Allegory is subdued to a pleasure in imagery and story-telling and the reminders of responsibilities in the actual world are not abrasive. The work is a sport, but not infertile: the exuberant inventiveness of its language and plot are developed in the novels, chastened by a sense of the reality of people.

The Shaving of Shagpat is the one achieved work to harness Meredith's delight in free-flying fantasy, which mostly found issue in tales told to his friends or plans for works never to be written.[2] He sensed the intimate presence of fantasy in human lives—its expression in wishes, in dreams, and in the associative rather than rational action of the mind —and in his later novels he freely explores its pressure in the world of daily experience.

In *The Ordeal of Richard Feverel*, however, Meredith was engaged in a direct struggle with the materials of life. He was intensely secretive about his childhood circumstances and his intimate experience, in particular his first marriage to Mary Ellen Nicolls, Peacock's widowed daughter. In life, his determination to obliterate wounding memories led him to destroy letters, to maintain almost complete reticence even with close friends and to 'annihilate' his wife after she had left him, refusing to visit her when dying or, until the last moment, to allow their child Arthur to visit her. In his art, he wrestled repeatedly with autobiographical material (though without admitting its sources in his own life), reinterpreting relationships crucial to his own experience, such as those of father and son, husband and errant wife. And he performed a self-analysis as stringent as it was covert.

One recurrent image, invested with acutely painful emotion, is that of being stripped naked and exposed. However different the context, the image has an unvarying grimness whether it be the comic Countess in *Evan Harrington* having 'a sensation of nakedness' or Alvan, in *The Tragic Comedians*, tearing off the shirt of Nessus. The dread is Meredith's own: 'We should speak Truth at all seasons. But there is a good reason for wearing clothes besides the shivering at nakedness; & to speak truth in decent manner is the right precept' (Aristophanes Portfolio). 'In decent manner', for Meredith, involved equivocation.

Meredith's equivocal feelings towards his material could sometimes be expressed by the simple distancing act of turning it into fiction; at other times the need to mask more completely his emotional relationship to the work he was producing led him to a self-protective irony or a peculiar grandiloquence, a 'clothing' of ideas in words. 'At the period when nature is strongest in us we are least natural. The reason is simply, that in growing old we can no longer take the trouble to assume a character' (Maroon Notebook). But in his novels he also observed his primary precept of speaking 'truth at all seasons'.

A crucial theme in *Richard Feverel* is the variety of ways in which we evade emotional responsibility for what we know to be true: by donning a mask against the world, by maintaining comic distance, by showing wisdom about others (and thus concealing blindness about ourselves), by grandiose idealism. Sir Austin, Richard, Adrian, all adopt some of these expedients. Some at least of them are also Meredith's. *Richard Feverel* is written out of excruciating personal experience and Meredith does not always maintain art's unperturbed control: the book is eruptive, erratic, fiercely hugging and repudiating its subject matter while also capable of tender and limpid insight into the nature of love and into the relationship between father and son.

During 1857–8, while he was writing the novel, Meredith's

marriage was in process of disintegrating. He had married in 1849 at the age of 21, his wife Mary being then 28 and already widowed. The marriage was gradually destroyed by poverty, by the combative brilliance of both partners, by their competitive literary ambitions, and finally by Mary's love affair with Wallis, the young painter who had used Meredith as model for his 'Death of Chatterton'. In 1857 Mary was travelling with Wallis in Wales; she bore a child (assumed to be his) in 1858 and they left together for Capri. But the relationship broke up and she returned alone to England to live in increasing distress of mind until 1861. Meredith refused ever to see her again. A striking contrast between what he could admit in outer life and in art is seen in his reaction to Mary's death: 'When I entered the world again I found that one had quitted it who bore my name: and this filled my mind with melancholy recollections' (*Letters*, i, 42). This poignantly laconic statement is the only reference in his letters; his response in art was to be the searing complexity of 'Modern Love' with its alternation of hectic posturing and magnanimity. The distinction he makes between his own marriage and that in the poem shows his personal needs. 'Modern Love' increases the husband's external guilt and salves his humiliation by providing him with a mistress.

Meredith's mother died when he was five. The disintegration of Meredith's childhood relationship to his father and the breakdown of his marriage both brought personal humiliation as well as emotional bereavement. He was an only child, taught to think himself above the other tradesmen's sons in Portsmouth where his grandfather (who figures as the Great Mel in *Evan Harrington*) had a prosperous tailoring business and lived in considerable style. His father, handsome, unpractical, spent much time with his son and built up in him a sense of special destiny. But the business failed; Meredith's father went bankrupt and married his housekeeper; Meredith, now a ward in chancery, set off to school in Germany when he was thirteen. The relationship between father and son was never restored.

In 1858 Meredith found himself the solitary father of a beloved only son on whom he fastened all his affections. 'To know oneself is more a matter of will than of insight' (Maroon Notebook): Meredith knew himself fiercely, though he concealed much from others. His personal situation while he was writing *Richard Feverel* brought together his early emotional deprivation and his later disillusionment—which included a savage disillusionment with himself.

Only his art was still potential. *Farina*, written just before *Richard Feverel*, had shown the same delight in language and incident as *The Shaving of Shagpat* but it was less exquisitely balanced between pastiche and re-creation. He drew on his loved Rhine landscape but the medievalism of the story is not acutely judged. The remote burlesque must have seemed nugatory alongside his own searing experiences at the time. When he comes to write *Richard Feverel* there is an extraordinary extension of range. Nothing in his earlier work, either in verse or prose, prepares one for its complex and passionate scrutiny of human experience. Meredith now had something beyond literature to write about, something which had been felt ferociously in his own life.

His situation was akin to that of Lawrence in *Sons and Lovers*: both artists were drawing upon an experience not yet fully comprehended and the act of writing became the process of understanding. The works share a vivid particularity and intensity; they have an effect of improvisation even when most intricately patterned. In each of them there is a sense of characters living beyond the borders of the pages, and to be understood fully only in a world outside fiction. In both novels the understanding which comes to the artist seems the result of the work rather than something contained within it. It took ten years for Lawrence to see the strength of the case he had made for Morel; Meredith, in revising his novel for the 1878 edition, cut out material that made Sir Austin appear ridiculous.

The Ordeal of Richard Feverel has been read in many different ways: Justin McCarthy described it in the *Westminster Review* as 'A novel with a purpose' and complained that it did not teach a clear lesson; 'but as a mere novel of character, it would not be easy to speak too highly of the talents which it indicates'. It has also been read as a story of star-crossed lovers. W. R. Mueller sees it as a struggle between the doctrine of the fall of man and the idea of evolution (The Great Shaddock Dogma, the Magian conflict and the System, are titles within the work for these ideas). J. W. Morris calls it a New Comedy imperfectly controlled (though this is to miss the punning signification of 'new' in the novel: it is a new *kind* of comedy although it has a Terentian plot). It can also be read as an indictment of parental tyranny on a par with *The Way of All Flesh* and as a *roman à clef* to Meredith's own life.[3] There is some validity in each of these readings: but each makes one aspect of the novel its centre. This enforces an unequivocal and incisive pattern of meaning in a novel whose effects and suggestions are always janus-faced, shifting, kaleidoscopic.

Of the various elements in the novel the idea of evolution in particular was vital to Meredith, principally because it affected his attitude towards the function of the novel. In his view, influenced by Herbert Spencer, man's continuing evolution was now centred in 'more brain' and the novel must expand the reader's capacity to understand:

At present, I am aware, an audience impatient for blood and glory scorns the stress I am putting on incidents so minute, a picture so little imposing. An audience will come to whom it will be given to see the elementary machinery at work: who, as it were, from some slight hint of the straws, will feel the winds of March when they do not blow. To them will nothing be trivial, seeing that they will have in their eyes the invisible conflict going on around us, whose features a nod, a smile, a laugh of ours perpetually changes. And they will perceive, moreover,

> that in real life all hangs together: the train is laid in the lifting of an eyebrow, that bursts upon the field of thousands. They will see the links of things as they pass, and wonder not, as foolish people now do, that this great matter came out of that small one. (xxv; 233–4)

Meredith saw that evolution implies continuity as well as development. Each man's growth epitomises an evolutionary process which may be equally disastrous whether it is arrested at a purely animal, appetitive level or loses the nourishment of its primitive instinctual life. His insistence on the essential oneness of realism and idealism is his version in art of man's wholeness and ability to progress. Meredith distrusted scientific materialism. Sir Austin Feverel is a 'scientific humanist' (p. 233) who seeks to make his son a perfect expression of a system. He is to be the forerunner of a more perfect race (the scientific imagery of evolution is ironically countered by imagery of the fall: 'the great Shaddock dogma'). In his determinism Sir Austin must reject poetry, spontaneity, and all the aberrant individuality of men:

> Now surely there will come an age when the presentation of science at war with Fortune and the Fates, will be deemed the true epic of modern life; and the aspect of a scientific humanist who, by dint of incessant watchfulness, has maintained a System against those active forces, cannot be reckoned less than sublime . . . (xxv; 233)

Later in his career Meredith views with equal irony that other dilettante scientist, Sir Willoughby Patterne: in each case 'science' is an expression of the will to dominate rather than to explore the world.

It would seem a simple matter to tell 'the story' of the novel but even at its briefest it involves one in interpretation. Sir Austin, betrayed by his wife and dogged by a sense of a family curse, is determined to educate his son Richard according to a new 'system' which will make him incorruptible. He is to be kept from sexual looseness and given a private family education. The result is that Richard is brought up surrounded by admiration, particularly that of his young cousin, Clare, and his friend Ripton. Richard falls in love with a country girl, Lucy, while his father is seeking a suitable wife for him in London. They marry without Sir Austin's knowledge and the baronet cuts himself off from his son. Richard, longing to be reconciled with his father, obeys his instructions to stay in London apart from his wife. He is systematically exposed to temptation on Sir Austin's instructions and is finally seduced by Bella Mount, a demi-mondaine he has hoped to 'save'. Clare, meanwhile, realising the hopelessness of her love for Richard, has gone into a dutiful marriage with a suitor of her mother. Richard's scorn and the physical degradation of an unloving marriage lead her to suicide. Ashamed at having failed both Clare and Lucy, Richard leaves for Europe accompanied by the radical Lady Judith, with a grandiose scheme of saving Italy from the Austrians. Meanwhile Lucy has borne his son and been received by Sir Austin into the family home. At last Richard returns, brought to an ecstatic realisation of his responsibilities by hearing of his son's birth. But he commits himself to fight a duel on the information of an out-of-date letter from Bella Mount telling him of Lord Mountfalcon's designs on Lucy (which have come to nothing). Richard is wounded in the duel and Lucy, distracted by being kept from him, dies of brain-fever. The last words of the book, written by Lady Blandish, are: 'Have you noticed the expression in the eyes of blind men? That is just how Richard looks, as he lies there silent in his bed—striving to image her on his brain.' (xlv; 558)

As I have just summarised it, the story suggests a coherent if melodramatic tragic pattern: the idealistic hero who cannot understand the suffering of others is overwhelmed by suffering at last. (It also places Richard closer to the centre of the work than is accurate: in the total experience Sir Austin is quite as important as his son.) But the tragic ending has persistently perturbed readers. The simplest reason for this is probably the most important. We have been led to sympathise with Lucy throughout; her death is both pathetic and unexpected. In a book where the characters are persistently subjected to irony she is the one character who has remained unsatirised: an ideal being, gentle and strong. Her brain-fever is perfectly believable in psychosomatic terms after the arbitrary treatment to which Richard and Sir Austin have subjected her. Brain-fever—though not perhaps a medically accurate description—is a recognisable stress illness, related to enforced passivity in emotional crises. Victorian society too often idealised passiveness in women both within fiction and outside it. Charlotte Brontë's *Shirley* gives a precise and agonised account of the illness, suffered by Caroline Helstone when she sees herself doomed to a life of solitude because Robert Moore does not return her unspoken love.

Lucy's death is disquieting not because it is unlikely but because it suggests a whole new unstable world of personality. Lucy has been shown to be strong yet she at last gives way. If Richard had been killed in the duel this would have been an appropriate outcome of the 'knight-errantry' which directed so many of his actions. But Lucy's death suggests the 'immense debtorship' for the thing done: Richard is to be punished through the effect of his actions on others, the way his actions *change* Lucy. For this to be brought about the author must play the role of Providence.

Until the last chapter the narrator has been omnipresent, commenting, examining, twining himself with the displayed consciousnesses of his characters. But the final chapter recounting the disaster is assigned to the sympathetic Lady Blandish who simply records and suffers. The scintillatingly ironic narrator cannot encompass the direct feeling needed at the end. Just as his kinsman within the novel, the cynical Adrian, has been displaced as commentator by Lady Blandish in the second part of the work, so the narrator himself gives way to her. The self-protecting irony with which Meredith has masked his relationship to his work means that he cannot find a narrative tone for the conclusion except through the dramatic voice of Lady Blandish. This also releases him from any need to force home an unequivocal judgment. It leaves us balked of a hierarchy of blame, faced with the fact of loss.

Later in his career Meredith was to emphasise the 'instructively tragic' in human affairs.[4] But the end of *Richard Feverel* teaches no clear lesson. Like *Romeo and Juliet*, to which Meredith's earlier admirers were fond of comparing it, there is something malign and arbitrary about the conclusion which suggests the hand of Providence rather than human responsibility (though in each case there *is* a heavy human responsibility). Ironically, Sir Austin himself has attempted to 'play Providence' to his son. He discovers that Providence is not always benign, particularly to those who impersonate her. Yet the whole tendency of the work has been to deny the existence of any authority beyond human behaviour. The Magian conflict is a conflict between the 'two men' *within us*. The problem is formalised in an early set scene between 'a tinker and a ploughman, who think that God is always fighting with the devil which shall command the kingdoms of the earth'.[5] Adrian, the 'wise youth', takes his stand with the Gods. Humanity is

> a supreme ironic procession, with laughter of Gods in the background. Why not laughter of mortals also? Adrian had his laugh in his comfortable corner. He possessed peculiar attributes of a heathen God. He was a disposer of men: he was polished, luxurious, and happy—at their cost. (i; 8–9)

Richard says of him that he 'only knows a part of people . . . and not the best part'. His one positive action begins the rift between Lucy and Richard: he persuades Lucy that it is to Richard's good for him to go first to his father without her. As F. D. Curtin pointed out in 'Adrian Harley: the limits of Meredith's comedy', Adrian, the completely cynical observer who sees through men without understanding them, is comedy's representative in the book—and he becomes a commentary on the limitations of comedy.[6]

John W. Morris considers *Richard Feverel* to be aesthetically a failure because the end flouts 'principles of order' established within the book itself: the archetype of New Comedy (the young marriage against parental opposition), and the 'analogical promise of a happy ending' established by the rick-burning episode, where the characters act in ways similar to those which produce the catastrophic conclusion.[7] But this is to flatten and resolve precisely what is energetic and equivocal in Meredith's handling of plot. Like Thackeray in *Vanity Fair*, Meredith is not just repeating well-known literary forms, nor even composing variations on them; he invokes them as emblems, as possible but limited ways of looking at his world. He discards them as his characters move into experiences not within the compass of, say, Menander's comedy. He counterpoints literary patterns against life, in which similar behaviour in different circumstances does *not* offer any 'analogical' assurance of a happy ending. So he crowds up the 'New Comedy' into the first third of the book.

The chapter in which the marriage of Richard and Lucy takes place is entitled 'In Which The Last Act Of A Comedy Takes The Place Of The First'. The marriage itself takes up only two pages at the end and is described in exclamatory abstractions (Time, Man, Woman, Angels, Devils) which shift in the distance from somewhat strident ecstasy to veiled comedy—in the midst of the solemnity Richard cannot find the ring and seizes one from the finger of his nurse.

Their hands are joined: their blood flows as one stream. Adam and fair Eve front the generations. Are they not lovely? Purer fountains of life were never in two bosoms.

And then they loose their hands, and the cool curate doth bid the Man to put a ring on the Woman's fourth finger, counting thumb.

And the Man thrusts his hand into one pocket, and into another, forward and back many times: into all his pockets. He remembers that he felt for it, and felt it in his waistcoat pocket, when in the Gardens. And his hand comes forth empty. And the Man is ghastly to look at! (xxix; 300–1)

The mock-biblical language of the second paragraph still has undertones of Genesis: but now the Man and the Woman are divested of their individuality without being made universal: the actions are described mechanistically ('the Man thrusts his hand into one pocket, and into another, forward and back many times: into all his pockets'.) The language of the bible has become mechanical and meaningless, something to be intoned by the cool curate: the Garden of Eden is now social Kensington Gardens.

The effect is comic, yet menacing. What should have been the lyric climax of the book if it were to be a comedy of happy endings is distanced to the point of diminution and the main part of the chapter is concerned with Clare's feelings: Clare, the undemonstrative cousin, who has loved Richard with poignant hopelessness throughout her life. The story of Clare, intertwining with Richard's life yet isolated from him, gives a trend towards sadness even during the boyhood chapters, when the unthinking buoyant comedy of Richard's brush with Farmer Blaize is played out. Indignant because Blaize has struck him for a poaching misdemeanour, Richard arranges with Tom the ploughman to fire the farmer's ricks. Tom is arrested and falls under threat of transportation: on that occasion all ends well. Richard swallows his pride and confesses to Farmer Blaize; Sir Austin who has secretly watched the progress of the whole affair feels his System confirmed; Tom is bound in gratitude to Richard. But the sore is really only skinned over: Richard is confirmed in his good opinion of himself by his generosity to Tom and the episode suggests that ill deeds can be put right by graceful apologies. This early incident is far from providing an optimistic pattern which we should expect later events to follow. It suggests, rather, how Richard and Sir Austin gratify themselves: Sir Austin by playing secret watcher and manipulator, Richard by chivalric behaviour in which humiliation feeds pride.

In *Richard Feverel* one of the most persistent of Meredith's creative irritations is expressed for the first time: the asperity with which he looks at his own experience. He views his own past enthusiasms with placing irony while at the same time he continues to express their uninhibited lyric wonder. First novels often call heavily on autobiographical experience: Meredith's novel is remarkable for the extent to which he handles such materials as if they were literature. He often finds a possible artistic relationship to his material by viewing it from the point of view contrary to his own in life. He uses literary models to provide a form for his fiction while at the same time he points out the limits of literary patterns. In *Richard Feverel*, for example, the education novel with its inherently optimistic assumptions is invoked. He draws on both *Emile*, with its concern for natural growth, and on Bulwer Lytton's *The Caxtons* with its sentimental account of a father's organised upbringing of a son (the father in Bulwer's novel is also called Austin).

These methods allow him both insight and superiority, an amalgam which was necessary in his earlier years if he was to create at all and which he only fitfully surpassed as he strove towards the larger, less self-protective vision of his maturity. In *Richard Feverel* the motives of system-makers are probed afresh. The relationship between 'nature' and 'science' is examined in evolutionary terms: What elements build a good man? how far is a new ideal of sexual behaviour attainable? how far can the personality be manipulated without impoverishment? The novel suggests no simple pattern of answers. It mirrors the opposing possibilities of human nature to which Meredith will offer no key. Richard Feverel is 'original man': his relationship to Lucy is paradisal: they are 'Adam and Eve' as well as 'Ferdinand and Miranda'; love is the 'Apple Disease'. Sir Austin is mistaken in subscribing to the 'Shaddock Dogma' (a primitive christianity which sees woman as the source of the fall) while at the same time playing the up-to-date scientist who can improve on natural selection.

Meredith drew two different kinds of material from his own life: he called upon his childhood experience and he scrutinised his juvenilia. In the Maroon Notebook meanwhile, he composed his own 'Pilgrim's Scrip', using some of the material in the novel, but continuing to assign sayings to 'Sir A. Fev.' after the book was published. *The Ordeal of Richard Feverel* is Meredith's method of distancing and dominating his experience in order that it may cease to threaten him; the aphoristic volume 'The Pilgrim's Scrip' is Sir Austin's protection from the practical application of his wisdom. The material in the Maroon Notebook makes clear Meredith's mordant jest at his own expense—his secret recognition that in large measure he *is* Sir Austin. He is Sir Austin not only because he is Sir Austin's creator and in an emotional predicament close to his, but even more because their parallel methods of recording and ordering experience spring from similar impulses of personality. The Maroon Notebook throngs with impersonal aphorisms; many are used in the novel where they are scrutinised in a dramatic context and commented on by the narrator. Others remain unpublished.

Meredith's notebooks abstract his own personal experience into general comments. Sir William Hardman recounted how, on a walking holiday in May 1862, 'Meredith overhauled his notebooks and read to me a number of aphorisms hereafter to be published in "The Pilgrim's Scrip", by Sir Austin Feverel, edited by Adrian Harley'.[8] This was three years after the publication of *Richard Feverel*. The remark assigned in the notebook to 'Sir A. Fev.' is 'We want a God to correct the horrible vindictiveness of Nature'.

The Maroon Notebook seems to have been in use from about 1858 to late 1862 (although it includes aphorisms which appear in works as late as *Beauchamp's Career*, 1875, and *Diana of the Crossways*, 1885). In 'The Pilgrim's Scrip', Meredith satirised his own private methods of recording experience but the 'Scrip' is also shown to be wise. He continued his own lapidary collections throughout his life: the satire does not result in a change of method or creativity.

His use of his early manuscript poems in the book, on the other hand, allows him to disown responsibility for them and bid farewell to their sentiments while giving them a kind of authority within the work. Phyllis Bartlett in 'Richard Feverel: Knight Errant' (*Bulletin of the New York Public Library*, lxiii, 1959) has shown that the poems assigned to Richard *and* to Sandoe, in *Richard Feverel*, are taken from Meredith's own early work. They represent, she suggests, a chivalric impulse in Richard's life which Meredith examines so savagely because he identified it with the impulse which had led to his own marriage with Mary: he, the young knight, she, the widow to be saved from the world. She quotes, from the diary of Clare in *Richard Feverel*:

> Thy truth to me is truer
> Than horse, or dog, or blade:
> Thy vows to me are fewer
> Than ever maiden made.
>
> Thou steppest from thy splendour
> To make my life a song:
> My bosom shall be tender
> As thine has risen strong.

Professor Bartlett points out that

> The first of these two stanzas is to be found in a serious collection of early manuscripts, dating shortly after the publication of his first Poems, as is the entire lyric, 'Might I lie where leans her lute', that Adrian mocked for its chastity.

Meredith is not simply mocking his own early work. The radical alienation of father and son begins when Sir Austin forces Richard to burn his own poems: 'Not only his blossoms withered, his being seemed to draw in its shoots and twigs' (xii; 102). Poetry's representative in the book is Diaper Sandoe, the contemptible poetaster who has run off with Sir Austin's wife and whom Meredith endows with his own early work. But Sir Austin, the scientific humanist, is unable to make a proper distinction between Sandoe and poetry itself—he feels threatened by poetry's independence. His own language, as the narrator indicates, is both the most poetic in the book and the most irresponsible:

> To talk nonsense, or poetry, or the dash between the two, in a tone of profound sincerity, and to enunciate solemn discordances with received opinion so seriously as to convey the impression of a spiritual insight, is the peculiar gift by which monomaniacs, having first persuaded themselves, contrive to influence their neighbours, and through them to make conquest of a good half of the world, for good or for ill. Sir Austin had this gift. He spoke as if he saw the truth, and, persisting in it so long, he was accredited by those who did not understand him, and silenced them that did. (xii; 99–100)

'There is nothing like a theory for blinding the wise', comments the narrator. The narrator himself *appears* uncommitted, the book undirective, despite its concern with 'problems of the day' such as the 'wild oats' theory, evolution, the plight of fallen women. The effect is prismatic: a multitude of points of view are presented, values shift, and the narrator's relationship to his characters is devious and inconstant. Sir Austin's most destructive error is to 'shut his heart and mask his face' (xxxiii; 347). The author is omnipresent but his face too is masked and the disconcerting effect of the work as a whole comes from his refusal to present consistent commentary or apportion blame definitively. He forces us to synthesise our own meaning for the book and presents us with an experience as strenuously unresolved as any in life.

The book's rapid, extreme and sometimes uncontrolled shifts of tone derive in part from Meredith's fierce closeness to his material and from his wish to dominate it. This wish is felt by artist and monomaniac alike and is akin to Sir Austin's will. The devious relationship between incident and presentation sometimes evades judgment, sometimes asserts values not dramatised in the characters. Style becomes the medium of judgment and, equally, of by-passing judgment. The style defines the world of the novel and Meredith's peculiar attitude to it. It is a style variously scintillating, ironic, naturalistic in dialogue, and percussive in its juxtaposition of lyric and deflationary language. In *Richard Feverel*, as Virginia Woolf observed, Meredith 'was at great pains to destroy the conventional form of the novel'.[9] His method of shaping the book was not based primarily on narrative sequence but on intermeshing incongruities of experience and feeling and dramatising their variety through the variety of his style.

This suggests the source of many readers' unease with the book: our sympathies are constantly engaged and interrupted, our interest deflected into new channels, and a kind of double focus used which allows the mind no point of rest. The effect is particularly striking when Meredith is writing about characters such as Sir Austin, Richard and Adrian, with whom he felt a covert and self-punishing identification. Occasionally he does show action and feeling fused. At moments when his characters come momentarily into accord, the style is limpid as in this scene between Sir Austin and Richard in his boyhood:

> It was a strange meeting. They seemed to have been separated so long. The father took his son's hand; they sat without a word passing between them. Silence said most. The boy did not understand his father: his father frequently thwarted him: at times he thought his father foolish: but that paternal pressure of his hand was eloquent to him of how warmly he was beloved. He tried once or twice to steal his hand away, conscious it was melting him. (ix; 76)

The short sentences; the repeated 'father'; the universality of 'father' and 'son'; the particular small acts ('The father took the son's hand'); all these express harmonious resolution through a simple, ritualised language. Such consistency of tone is rare. More often the narration dramatises conflicting attitudes: the conflict is sometimes felt by the characters, but often it is between the character and the narrative or even within the narrative itself.

In the first chapter of the revised edition, for instance, we are presented with a dourly succinct description of the break up of Sir Austin's marriage. 'He had a wife and he had a friend.'

> Such was the outline of the story. But the baronet could fill it up. He had opened his soul to these two. He had been noble Love to the one, and to the other perfect Friendship. He had bid them be brother and sister whom he loved, and live a Golden Age with him at Raynham. In fact, he had been prodigal of the excellences of his nature, which it is not good to be, and, like Timon, he became bankrupt, and fell upon bitterness.
>
> . . . .
>
> After five years of marriage, and twelve of friendship, Sir Austin was left to his loneliness with nothing to ease his heart of love upon save a little baby boy in a cradle. (i; 3)

The succession of simple statements is presented as Sir Austin's summarised consciousness, but the literary references derive from the narrator. Shakespeare and Keats are invoked. Sir Austin is connected to a tragic hero (Timon) and to the gods:

> And all those acts which Deity supreme
> Doth ease its heart of love in
>
> (*Hyperion*, Bk. I)

The changing tenses both suggest and blur the shift from Sir Austin's view to that of the narrator. 'In fact, he had been prodigal of the excellences of his nature'—the summarising 'In fact' suggests the narrator's placing survey but the pluperfect retains the tense which has been used for Sir Austin's epitomised consciousness; 'which it is not good to be'—the present tense generalises the statement so that it carries the authority of the narrator as well as representing Sir Austin's opinion; 'and, like Timon, he became bankrupt, and fell upon bitterness'—the tense shifts anew, to the preterite, and is now unequivocally the narrator's commentary and interpretation.

The flexible movement from character to narrator is neither entirely ironic, nor entirely sympathetic. Just as in the preceding paragraph Lady Feverel and Diaper Sandoe have been compared to those least appealing lovers, Rizzio and Mary, so here Sir Austin is identified with the narrowest of tragic heroes, Timon. A more generous reference is used when Sir Austin is described 'easing his heart of love' on the 'little baby boy in a cradle': the allusion allows Sir Austin's plight its full stature. But by the lofty parallels the narrator (also) suggests that Sir Austin himself sees his fate in grandiloquent terms, and that his godlike stance, his qualities of Love and Friendship, his invocation of a Golden Age, are aspects of the grandiose egoism which has driven the lovers from him. His self-consciousness is suggested by the use of capital letters, and the typography represents Sir Austin's orotund speech: Love, Friendship, a Golden Age. The paragraph is both poignant and comic. The two qualities can exist together because there is no sharp division between narrator and character, while at the same time the shifting tenses, the allusions, the capitalising make it clear that a division does exist.

The book's narrative method is akin to Sir Austin's own manner: it masks opaqueness with wisdom. Take the scene where Sir Austin has heard of Richard's marriage:

'The God of this world is in the machine—not out of it', Sir Austin interrupted her [Lady Blandish], and pressed her hand to get the good-night over.

At any other time her mind would have been arrested to admire the phrase; now it seemed perverse, vain, false, and she was tempted to turn the meaning that was in it against himself, much as she pitied him.

'You know, Emmeline', he added, 'I believe very little in the fortune, or misfortune, to which men attribute their successes and reverses. They are useful impersonations to novelists; but my opinion is sufficiently high of flesh and blood to believe that we make our own history without intervention. Accidents?—Terrible misfortunes?—What are they?—Good-night.'

'Good-night', she said, looking sad and troubled. 'When I said, "misfortune", I meant, of course, that he is to blame, but—shall I leave you his letter to me?'

'I think I have enough to meditate upon', he replied, coldly bowing.

'God bless you', she whispered. 'And—may I say it? do not shut your heart.'

He assured her that he hoped not to do so, and the moment she was gone he set about shutting it as tight as he could.

If, instead of saying, Base no system on a human being, he had said, Never experimentalize with one, he would have been nearer the truth of his own case. . . . A Manichæan tendency, from which the sententious eulogist of nature had been struggling for years (and which was partly at the bottom of the System), now began to cloud and usurp dominion of his mind. As he sat alone in the forlorn dead-hush of his library, he saw the devil.

How are we to know when we are at the head and fountain of the fates of them we love?

There by the springs of Richard's future, his father sat: and the devil said to him: 'Only be quiet: do nothing: resolutely do nothing: your object now is to keep a brave face to the world, so that all may know you superior to this human nature that has deceived you. For it is the shameless deception, not the marriage, that has wounded you.'

'Ay!' answered the baronet, 'the shameless deception, not the marriage! wicked and ruinous as it must be; a destroyer of my tenderest hopes! my dearest schemes! Not the marriage:—the shameless deception!' and he crumpled up his son's letter to him, and tossed it into the fire.

How are we to distinguish the dark chief of the Manichæans when he talks our own thoughts to us? (xxxiii; 343–5)

The scene shows Meredith's artistry at its most subtle: the syntax of the dialogue expresses the characters as surely as their sentiments. Sir Austin uses a series of completed, logically connected statements. He invokes the interrogative to close questions, not to raise them—while Lady Blandish gropes her way towards the truth of what she means through half-completed sentences and exclamations. Meredith does not fall into the easy convention, common to Victorian novelists even as good as Mrs Gaskell, of making everyone talk alike when under pressure of emotion, in a biblical rhetoric which confidently expects a wholehearted response from the reader. Rather he heightens the quiddities of speech and offsets them against small emblematic actions interpreted by the narrator: he 'pressed her hand to get the good-night over'. In this scene he uses the shift from dialogue to indirect speech to represent the shutting of Sir Austin's heart. 'He assured her that he hoped not to do so . . .'

The narrative commentary which follows seems to be a straightforward intervention by the omniscient author: Sir Austin is placed as 'the sententious eulogist of nature', the System is 'a Manichæan tendency'. But with the Shakespearean imagery 'to cloud and usurp dominion of his mind' the mood shifts.

> As he sat alone in the forlorn dead-hush of his library, he saw the devil.
>
> How are we to know when we are at the head and fountain of the fates of them we love?

The force of the statement 'he saw the devil' derives partly from its poetic concreteness after the rather abstract vocabulary earlier in the paragraph, partly from its grammatical directness. It is presented absolutely, in time and place ('the forlorn dead-hush of his library'), with no hint of whimsicality. The whole tendency of the book has been towards ironic, light-weight labels—'the Eighteenth Century', 'the

Blossoming Period'—so that the sombre absoluteness of the psycho-religious term 'the devil' comes as a shock which opens the reader's imagination. And the poignant question (set alone): 'How are we to know when we are at the head and fountain of the fates of them we love?' speaks directly to us, appealing to our experience outside the world of fiction, which is here made meaningful by the example of Sir Austin. Sir Austin's inner debate is rendered through hypnotically re-iterated phrases such as 'the shameless deception, not the marriage' which move from rationalisation to incantation. His purpose is shown to be not debate but self-endorsement.

'How are we to distinguish the dark chief of the Manichæans when he talks our own thoughts to us?' is the second question the narrator asks. Again the reader is poised between the clarity with which Sir Austin's errors are demonstrated and the enforced recognition that we, as much as he, do not know what is within us unless it is demonstrated to us through art. But the second question raises other problems about the meaning of the book.

The passage quoted, with its complicated meshing of naturalistic dialogue, emblematic action, formalised inner consciousness and extending commentary, *contains* the irony which more commonly flashes on the narrative surface. It is here implicit in the contrast between words and deeds: the Baronet can formulate wisdom but not apply it to himself. He, who has 'wished to be Providence to his son' (iv; 35) (so his actions are described by Adrian), in theory recognises that 'we make our own history without intervention'. The *commentary* of the book seems to endorse Sir Austin's belief in personal responsibility rather than in the novelist's 'useful impersonation', 'the dark chief of the Manichæans'. Yet the *action* of the novel, though expressed in human terms, is Manichæan—in the fight between God and the Devil it is the devil who triumphs and destroys.

Richard, the original man, becomes fallen man not

through his pre-lapsarian relationship to Lucy but through his god-like father's System for perfecting him: a System which, emphasising integrity, has left no place for self-doubt or self-examination. Sir Austin has tried to strengthen Richard to meet the family's hereditary 'ordeal' and to avoid the curse of the Feverels: he sees his as a special fate, a special curse. The knightly ordeal is traditionally a test of courage and endurance: but Sir Austin fails to recognise that an ordeal of suffering such as he has undergone is common to all men, not the result of a peculiar curse. The taint of the Feverels is pride, and this again makes the family simply representative of mankind: the education Sir Austin gives Richard disastrously reinforces his pride and his sense of being a prince marked out for a special providence.

The allegory is tortuously woven into the narrative by means of emblematic names and references. When Meredith revised the novel for the 1878 edition he removed some vagaries of tone at the expense of obscuring the double-edged significance of the Ordeal, and of the knightly training which Richard had undergone.

The cuts to the first edition condense the book's opening. The original version begins with a burlesque description of the numerous ladies attracted to Sir Austin's household by the publication of his sententious and misogynistic Pilgrim's Scrip. Women, it is implied, like to be mastered and seen through and are attracted by those they would convert. 'Woman when she wrestles for supremacy with every one she encounters, is but seeking her Master', writes Sir Austin in 'The Pilgrim's Scrip'.[10] 'Women have a strong tendency to adore great men and make little men' or 'Woman is what man makes her, and man what woman will let him be', writes Meredith in the Maroon Notebook. The farcical 'Femmes Savantes' disappear from the later version: Lady Blandish's name, the only survival from the vein of mock eighteenth-century comedy, loses all significance as the book proceeds. The other major deletion is the encounter between Sir Austin and Mrs Grandison and again the eighteenth-century references are dropped. Mrs Grandison, who models her behaviour on Richardson's hero, is a more ridiculous, because more self-satisfied, female counterpart of Sir Austin: both are seeking the perfect moral match for their offspring—and their ponderous deliberations heighten the idyll of young love between Richard and Lucy.

Perhaps Meredith recognised that the heavy anti-feminine jibes were more important to his own emotional needs while he was writing the book than they were to his main themes. The novel itself outgrows them, as its creator came to perceive. The savage summary of the life of the lovers, Lady Feverel and Diaper Sandoe, is, however, retained in the revised versions. Lady Feverel is so wraith-like a being that her 'rescue' by Richard—the one achievement among all his grandiose projects—remains totally unreal. It is also quite uncritically presented. In *The Egoist* (which Meredith was writing at about the time he was revising *Richard Feverel* for the edition of 1878) he sardonically creates for Sir Willoughby similar revenge fantasies about Clara's fate.

In *Richard Feverel* it is the narrator himself who creates the humiliated Diaper Sandoe and Lady Feverel.

One may suppose that a prematurely aged, oily little man; a poet in bad circumstances; a decrepit butterfly chained to a disappointed ink-stand, will not put out strenuous energies to retain his ancient paramour when a robust young man comes imperatively to demand his mother of him in her person. The colloquy was short between Diaper Sandoe and Richard. The question was referred to the poor spiritless lady, who seeing that her son made no question of it, cast herself on his hands. (xxxviii; 430–1)

In *The Egoist* the narrator recounts ironically Sir Willoughby's fantasies, in which he imagines Clara humiliated:

Contemplating her in the form of a discarded weed, he had a catch of the breath: she was fair. He implored his Power that Horace de Craye might not be the man! Why any man? An illness, fever, fire, runaway horses, personal disfigurement, a laming, were sufficient. And then a formal and noble offer on his part to keep to the engagement with the unhappy wreck: yes, and to lead the limping thing to the altar, if she insisted. His imagination conceived it, and the world's applause besides. (xxix; 356)

The design of *Richard Feverel* is baroque in its proliferation of ornament: its surface is richly encrusted with epigrams and ideas. Intellectual notions run through the book at varying levels of seriousness: commitment to 'the Age', idealised in the character of Richard's cousin Austin and grappled with in Richard's own idealistic misadventures; the 'Magian conflict', which is variously presented as theological dualism or as the struggle between nature and science; ideas of evolution and of natural selection. Richard is the 'new man' but he is restored to manhood by becoming a father, not by his idealistic aspirations. Sir Austin, the 'scientific humanist', who has 'nursed the Devil', forces the most natural of actions into his rigid System: he will not allow Lucy to cease breast-feeding when she is distraught with grief during Richard's illness because of his theories of the efficacy of mother's milk. Meredith himself was an ardent believer in breast-feeding—here it is Sir Austin's theorizing authoritarianism that is being attacked.

We see the same fecundity and intricacy of imaginative design in the numerous commenting characters. The cynically disengaged 'Wise Youth', Adrian, even distances himself from his own epigrams by adopting a fustian language to indicate that life is a bad play deserving no serious attention or involvement:

'Well, all wisdom is mournful. 'Tis therefore, coz, that the wise do love the Comic Muse. Their own high food would kill them. You shall find great poets, rare philosophers, night after night on the broad grin before a row of yellow lights and mouthing masks. Why? Because all's dark at home.' (vi; 48)

He is the supremely successful 'masker', or 'masquer' in a work preoccupied with the destructiveness of masks; because he has no heart to distort or enhance his perceptions he is able to present in summary form truths that the other characters must live out in passionate experience. While Richard is still a boy Adrian cites a poem of Diaper Sandoe and comments in an argument with his cousin Austin on radicalism and Work:

> 'Consider that phrase, "Ophelia of the Ages"! Is not Brawnley . . . just the metaphysical Hamlet to drive her mad? She, poor maid! asks for marriage and smiling babes, while my lord lover stands questioning the Infinite, and rants to the Impalpable.' (vi; 49)

The comment reverberates through the later action of the book.

Mrs Berry, Richard's totally sympathetic nurse, is the opposite moral extreme from Adrian.[11] She was banished from Raynham when Richard was still a baby because one night she saw the face behind the 'flexible mask' of Sir Austin's features:

> She could hardly believe her senses to see the austere gentleman, dead silent, dropping tear upon tear before her eyes. She lay stone-still in a trance of terror and mournfulness, mechanically counting the tears as they fell, one by one. The hidden face, the fall and flash of those heavy drops in the light of the lamp he held, the upright, awful figure, agitated at regular intervals like a piece of clock-work by the low murderous catch of his breath: it was so piteous to her poor human nature that her heart began wildly palpitating. Involuntarily the poor girl cried out to him, 'Oh, sir!' and fell a-weeping. (i; 4–5)

The poignant contrast between human machine ('mechanically', 'regular intervals', 'a piece of clockwork') and human agony is resolved momentarily in her cry. Her later role in the novel is a rather unsatisfactory combination of pungent homeliness and sentiment which, drawing on such models as Juliet's nurse, often seems forced and literary, unspontaneous. This is so, for instance, in the irritating complication that she should turn out to be the abandoned wife of Berry, Sir Austin's man-servant. It makes a too-neat comic counter to Sir Austin's situation and a confusingly reductive parallel to Lucy. She is kin to those images of folk-wisdom and folk-assumptions of Meredith's later work, Dame Nature (*One of Our Conquerors*) and Dame Gossip (*The Amazing Marriage*).

The juggling with notions and language gives an effect both exuberant and hectic: as readers we are emotionally involved and repudiated. Yet the crises are intensely poignant—and this poignancy is achieved by simple, detailed description. Richard fondles a leveret as he walks through the storm-swept forest after hearing of the birth of his son (in such scenes we see how naturally Lawrence drew upon Meredith's inspiration):

> He was next musing on a strange sensation he experienced. It ran up one arm with an indescribable thrill, but communicated nothing to his heart. It was purely physical, ceased for a time, and recommenced, till he had it all through his blood, wonderfully thrilling. He grew aware that the little thing he carried in his breast was licking his hand there. The small rough tongue going over and over the palm of his hand produced the strange sensation he felt. Now that he knew the cause, the marvel ended; but now that he knew the cause, his heart was touched and made more of it. (xlii; 522)

Lucy is left without explanation by Richard immediately after his homecoming (he has gone to the duel): 'baby cried vehemently, and Lucy, sobbing, took him and danced him and sang to him with drawn lips and tears dropping over him' (xliv; 553).

The unstable shifting between levity, fierce thought, high-spirited humour, garish drama, lyricism and integrity of insight makes *Richard Feverel* a troubling experience. Meredith himself explained his attitude to Sir Austin's System ('The moral is that no System of the sort succeeds with human nature, unless the originator has conceived it purely independent of personal passion') and claimed 'contrast' as an ordering principle in the book ('I did not insist on it and lecture my dear public. I thought providing a contrast sufficient—in the "Unmasking of Ripton Thompson"').[12] But 'contrast' is both too stable and too static a term for the richly erratic variations which Meredith plays upon his obsessive emotional themes in the book.

Meredith watched himself distrustfully as he entered into Sir Austin's situation in his own life. 'Proverbs—the use and creation of them a sign of narrowness', writes Meredith in the Maroon Notebook; 'A maker of Proverbs—what is he but a narrow mind the mouthpiece of a *narrower*?', writes Sir Austin in '*the old Note-book*' (xliv; 536, my italics). The entries in the Maroon Notebook (which Meredith continued to use for at least three years after he had completed *Richard Feverel*) show how his thoughts pursue the problems which preoccupy or are demonstrated by Sir Austin—for example: 'Is it not cowardly to lay all our sins at the door of the devil?'; 'We can trace our misfortunes to one weakness: but we cannot see that the previous course of our life produced it'. And 'The visible Devil is Ignorance: & Humanity's first want is more Brain'; 'The wishes we secretly nurse are the fathers of our future.'

This secret kinship between author and character is part of a complex interlocking which is never resolved; at times the two overlap, sometimes they polarize, but always they are interdependent. Sir Austin is the reader's chief guide as well as his prey in reading the book. The strain the book imposes on us as readers comes ultimately from the impossibility of setting Sir Austin at a stable distance (even to the extent that we can set Richard apart from us).

In *The Egoist* Meredith is authoritatively separated from Sir Willoughby by the act of creating him—which involves an intelligence and self-knowledge of which Willoughby is incapable. With Sir Austin there is no such final separation: Sir Austin, capable of insight and wisdom, but incapable of their practical application, is closer to Meredith's own situation. Frequently, criticism of Sir Austin conceals emotional sympathy with his attitude—particularly with his misogynistic view of marriage.[13] Meredith's letters at this period show how bitter was his disillusionment with women and with sexual love. 'Intense love is a violation of life', he wrote in the Blue Notebook at this time. His confidence in his power to understand women had been deeply shaken by his personal experience. The heroines in the book, though robustly alive and actual, correspond completely to traditional *types* of womanhood. The fair, passive Lucy is, moreover, the furthest one can imagine from Mary's scintillating personality. Within the novel the figure who shares Mary's brilliance is the attractive and depraved Bella Mount. The idealisation of Lucy is not simply a weakness in the book, to be explained, if scarcely excused, by biographical evidence. Her presence prevents the novel from lapsing into easy misogyny. Meredith's invocation of her shows the generous commitment to a character's experience which enlarges his vision and which is one of the richest veins in his artistic individuality. Through the ideal figure of Lucy the book exorcises the bitterness shared by Meredith and Sir Austin but it still requires her to be sacrificed.

No way out of the pattern of marital loss is shown within the novel—even the idealised cousin Austin Wentworth and the earthy Mrs Berry suffer broken marriages. The conclusion tragically reiterates the pattern drawn from Meredith's twice repeated experience in life (as child and husband). Richard, like Sir Austin before him, is left, solitary, with an only son.

2

The Adventures of Harry Richmond The Education of Romance: a Role for the Narrator

IN his response to the novel form Meredith was caught between his belief in the public function of the novel and his sense of his own special strengths. Henry James said of Meredith after his death that the artist was always subservient to the good citizen.[1] Yet when a conflict arose between the novel as a force for education and his own introspective devotion to nicety of perception, Meredith was content to be obscure rather than blunt his meaning. He thought that art must cure and educate: 'Art is the specific' (*Egoist*, Prelude). It would *enrich* mankind by expanding consciousness. Art which seeks to cure is likely to be didactic or satiric; Meredith's work however goes beyond corrective comedy to include the ideal possibilities within human relationships. If his art is to help man's moral evolution he must interest a large audience, for whom his probing of the deeper levels of motive will be a discovery involving self-discovery. Writing to Jessopp on 20 September 1864 he says of the volume of poems which included 'Modern Love':

> A man who hopes to be popular, must think from the mass, and as the heart of the mass. If he follows out vagaries of his own brain, he cannot hope for general esteem; and he does smaller work. (*Letters*, i, 156)

But although Meredith wished for popularity so that his work could attain its full significance he would not turn to more orthodox artistic methods when this involved subordinating his characters to perfected plot. It was essential to his view of the novel's purpose that the growth of personality should be its central theme and that this growth should not appear to end with the book.

Writing to Maxse in 1865 he said:

> Hawthorne has just the pen to fascinate you. His deliberate analysis, his undramatic representations, the sentience rather than the drawings which he gives you of his characters, and the luscious, morbid tone, are all effective. But I think his delineations untrue: their power lies in the intensity of his egotistical perceptions, and are not the perfect view of men and women. (*Letters*, i, 168)

His description of Hawthorne's work reveals a half-acknowledged fascination. This is particularly remarkable since the letter was written while Meredith was at work on *Vittoria*, the novel which represented his most determined attempt to move away from his earlier analytical method towards the epic: 'The softer emotions are not kept at half gasp upon slowly-moving telescopic objects, with their hearts seen beating in their frames' (*Letters*, i, 169). In his next letter he is clearly answering Maxse's observation of the kinship between Meredith's own method and that of Hawthorne:

> As regards Hawthorne, little Meredith admits that your strokes have truth. I strive by study of humanity to represent it: not its morbid action. I have a tendency to do that, which I repress: for, in delineating it, there is no gain. In all my, truly, very faulty works, there is this aim. Much of my strength lies in painting morbid emotion and exceptional positions; but my conscience will not let me so waste my time. Hitherto consequently I have done nothing of mark. But I shall, and 'Vittoria' will be the first indication (if not fruit) of it. My love is for epical subjects—not for cobwebs in a putrid corner; though I know the fascination of unravelling them. (*Letters*, i, 171)

Meredith's recognition of his own tendencies was more accurate than his prophecy that his career would take wing when he drove his energies into the 'epical'. His talent for presenting character lay in the intricacy with which he was able to trace the psychological sources of action and explore the different levels of consciousness simultaneously at work. But his ideal of character was quite different: he admired large simple natures like Emilia in *Sandra Belloni* and Carinthia in *The Amazing Marriage*, and those who were able to practise self-abnegation without rancour—such as the silent, prematurely middle-aged men who finally win his later heroines, Vernon Whitford, Thomas Redworth, Owain Wythan. As soon as he brought such natures into the focus of his magnifying glass, however, they dulled, or proved as sophistical as the rest of us. This troubled him throughout his career; he constantly tried out new solutions to the problem.

A related problem which beset him in the early books was that of finding a role for the narrator within the novel which would allow him to interpret without disrupting the fictional world. In the novels of the eighteen-sixties (in many ways the least successful of his career) we see him trying out a series of technical experiments which crystallise into the achievement of *Harry Richmond*.

In any narrative the presence of the author is inevitably implied in the story he chooses to tell, in the selection of episodes for narration or dramatisation, in the manipulation of time and place; and third-person narration suggests his presence as observer. Dialogue is most free of the author since it is happening *now*, whereas narrative enacts for us in the present what the tense affirms to be past and thus under the author's control. (The end of *Women in Love* shows the uses of dialogue: the arguments and affirmations of Birkin and Ursula are left unresolved and resonant, avoiding what might otherwise have seemed a merely didactic conclusion.)

The lyricism of Meredith's method, as well as his concern with psychological realism, gives a special importance to the role of the narrator. He rarely uses a single point of view to present his fiction, but the narrator's insistent presence, expressed in the style, controls the rapid shifts between irony and ecstasy, detachment and perturbation. He also uses interventions by the narrator and differing projections of the author's presence to intensify his relationship to the reader.[2]

Our principal means of growth, in his view, is to increase our consciousness. This brings with it a new awareness of complexity, while at the same time it gives access to more of the personality. The narrator's interventions heighten our awareness as readers; they are not moral directives. The interventions discuss *method*: the moral implications are dramatised in the contradictions between the character's motives and actions.

By the time he wrote *Sandra Belloni* (1864), the most experimental of his early novels, the analytical interpositions of the narrator had become the controlling device.

> A showman once (a novice in his art, or ambitious beyond the mark), after a successful exhibition of his dolls, handed them to the company, with the observation, 'Satisfy yourselves, ladies and gentlemen'. The latter, having satisfied themselves that the capacity of the lower limbs was extraordinary, returned them, disenchanted. That showman did ill. But I am not imitating him. I do not wait till after the performance, when it is too late to revive illusion. To avoid having to drop the curtain, I choose to explain an act on which the story hinges, while it is advancing: which is, in truth, an impulse of character. Instead of his being more of a puppet, this hero is less wooden than he was. Certainly I am much more in awe of him. (xiii; 113–14)

Thackeray is clearly the showman referred to here. Meredith's admiration for Thackeray (particularly for his portraits of women) was always tempered by his dislike and dread of the narrator who acts simply as 'puppeteer'.

Meredith's open discussion of technique within his novels is a part of his belief in free will.[3] This belief expresses itself in a number of ways: he gives character pre-eminence over shapeliness of plot; he flouts the analogues and expectations he has built up in the reader; he exploits comedy (with its emphasis on the accountability of individuals) and he invokes the comic spirit, which insists on observation rather than involvement from reader and narrator alike. He seeks our free assent to the implications of what he shows rather than a passing emotional submission to fiction. Meredith claims that to break dramatic illusion does not in the long run undermine our acceptance of his characters. We are able to relate them more meaningfully to our own experience because we have been made more alert to the methods by which we reach our own evaluations of character.

In his early work Meredith is not entirely confident that he can render the full complexity of his meaning. At times his appeals to posterity over the heads of his present readers exaggerate the novelty of what he is doing. As so often in Meredith's work, we are faced with a situation which can alternatively be seen as deriving from weakness or from strength. The interventions enable him to enlarge the scope of his work by confronting his technical weaknesses and turning them to fresh account. His 'Dd. Dd. Dd. uncertain workmanship' at least makes him test new means of expression instead of retreating into timidity.

Ford Madox Ford said that 'the trouble with English nuvvelists (*sic*) from Fielding to Meredith, is that not one of them cares whether you believe in their characters or not'.[4] Meredith clearly did care whether we believe in his characters but, like Fielding, he was not committed to formal realism. Both novelists were attempting to use fiction as a means to truth while acknowledging it as fiction. They both laid claim to being 'historians'. Meredith never suggests that he is in command of the fate of his characters or that he can alter the direction of the story. By his narrative interventions he breaks the illusion that there is one absolute way of rendering the world: the interventions complicate what may appear simple.

In comedy, which implies detachment, a consciousness of the author's presence is reassuring: it suggests that control is being maintained. The equivalence of promise and performance creates a benign universe. In tragedy, however, or an absorbing mode like the romance, the presence of the author may be felt as an intrusion, even an impertinence. The reader is led to question the necessity of what is shown, to consider how far it may be simply the author's whim at work. Hardy might seem to be the classic case of this but his use of chance is not an intrusion in this sense. If the use of coincidence and of ironic commentary suggest the manipulation of a malign author, that is, after all, the nature of the universe as Hardy conceives it. Hardy has seized the problem and elevated it into a creative principle. Meredith, whose central artistic method is equivocation, has no such way open to him. He seems uneasy about the overt presence of the author within his work (in contrast to Fielding's magnanimous assurance) and often takes up a defensive stance instead of engaging the reader's sympathy.

Meredith's elaborate style implies and distances the narrator with unusual force; he is never invisible though often dramatically masked. The direct presence of the author as narrator is increasingly subdued as his career goes on. In *Harry Richmond* the narrator is the hero—and neither narrator nor hero is Meredith. The first-person narration cuts the knot (a solution which he uses only in that one novel). Even in the early books, there are remarkable differences from novel to novel in the personality suggested and in his relationship with the reader. We can see the shift of narrative presence by taking the first four novels, *The Ordeal of Richard Feverel*, *Evan Harrington*, *Sandra Belloni*, *Rhoda Fleming*, each of which is inhabited by a subtly different narrator. In *Richard Feverel* the narrator emphasizes the allegorical level of the book and from time to time forces the reader to detach himself from the characters. He does this by assigning ironic defining titles to his characters and to periods in their lives, 'The Blossoming Period', 'The Magnetic Age'. These stiffen into comedy what to Richard is uncharted discovery. His references to his people as puppets—though all his endeavour is to release them from their puppet attitudes—chill the sympathies. The narrator seems stoically detached. Comedy is invoked, not as a total mode or as a reassurance, but as one way of looking, whose inadequacies the narrator perceives when he sets it against the complexities of experience. The narrator sometimes remarks directly on his people and their relevance to us (as in the chapter 'Nursing the Devil'): he is given to drawing apophthegms from the scenes he describes. Yet the effect created by this icy control is of a passionate and barely dominated personal involvement with his characters.

In *Evan Harrington* (1861), where Meredith is again autobiographically involved with his subject matter, he adopts a very different narrative tone. The manner here is one of social assurance, a certain heartiness which assumes that both author and reader can afford to laugh at the follies of aspiring young men. The narrator appears as a jovial 'I' and his half sympathetic, half condescending examination of Evan Harrington sets him at a safe comic distance from his characters. 'Our comedies are frequently youth's tragedies. We will smile reservedly as we mark Mr Evan Harrington's step into the midst of the fair society of the drawing room'.

Meredith may have used this button-holing manner partly because the novel was his first attempt to write concurrently with serialisation (it appeared in the popular magazine *Once a Week*, a rival to Dickens's *Household Words*). He had considerable difficulty with the serial method which, with its dependence on frequently repeated plot-crises and total dramatisation, was inimical to his purposes. Dickens, Reade and Collins, who wrote novels of sensational incident, evolved an empirical aesthetic of the 'dramatic novel' (in Reade's phrase). Dickens expressed it thus: 'My notion is that when I have made the people to play out the play, it is, as it were their business to do it and not mine'.[5]—One of the most remarkable shifts in the history of the novel is the process by which this idea, associated in the middle of the century with 'low-brow' novelists and combated by the more 'intellectual' analytical writers such as Thackeray, George Eliot and Meredith, became by the eighteen-nineties the creed of Henry James and for much of the twentieth century has remained the central ethic for the critical reading of fiction.

Meredith wrote that interest 'not to be false and evanescent, must kindle slowly, and ought to centre more in character—out of which incidents should grow'.[6] The humorous, confidential manner of the narrator—who promises his readers further revelations ('But that, for the moment, is my secret') and presents the scene as on a stage—is very different from that usually adopted by Meredith. It is an attempt to establish a relationship with his assumed audience which will sustain their amused concern despite the lack of melodramatic crises.[7]

But there is another reason for Meredith's carefully maintained distance from his characters and his self-consciously gentlemanly appeal to his readers. By the very act of writing the book Meredith was playing a role akin to that of the *parvenue* Countess in his novel. She conceals her family background; he concealed the autobiographical foundation of his story, which draws more immediately on family history than any other of his works. The 'Great Mel' of the novel, Melchizedec, deceased father of Evan and the Countess—is an exuberant gentleman tailor: he is drawn directly from the equally fantastic figure of Meredith's grandfather, also a gentleman tailor and actually called Melchizedeck. S. M. Ellis, a distant relative, showed (with some resentment) in his biography the extent to which Meredith had made use of his aunts and other relatives for the characters of *Evan Harrington*.[8] He had also used his family's snobbery and their refusal to acknowledge their origins in tailordom. It was a snobbery he shared and a social uncertainty which particularly beset him at the time of the composition of *Evan Harrington*. He had new aristocratic and liberal friends, the Duff Gordons. Their sixteen-year-old daughter Janet is presented in an unusually direct way as the heroine, Rose Jocelyn, and Meredith, then a widower in his thirties, was clearly in love with her.[9] Part of the exuberance of the portrait of the Countess undoubtedly derives from this private level of the book, which he was unable to share with any one. The Countess is in a socially precarious situation similar in some ways to that of Meredith himself and handling it with greater daring and panache. The buoyancy as well as the comparative shallowness of *Evan Harrington* derives from the gratified wish-fulfillment on which it is based: it is fed by the social assurance of the narrator, by the style and ultimately unrouted pride of the Countess, by the adventures of the hero who wins a lady's hand and restores her to fortune, rejecting the blandishments of the gentlemanly world and enjoying its advantages. The autobiographical elements in these first two novels to some extent explain Meredith's insistent use of very diverse narrative *personae*.

The direct autobiographical relevance drops away in *Sandra Belloni* (first published as *Emilia in England*). In this novel the narrator constantly intervenes in the guise of conscious artist and experimenter. Meredith was attempting to combine social satire and an exploration of the subconscious levels of personality. He had been disappointed that the structural contrasts which he used to suggest his meaning in *Richard Feverel* had been overlooked by critics and public alike: in *Sandra Belloni* he uses analytical interpolations to explain his methods, and also dramatises the novelty of his approach in the figure of the Philosopher who comments on the action from time to time.[10] The Philosopher is a caricature of Meredith as minute examiner of motive, but he differs ostensibly from Meredith in feeling no affection for the characters. The debate between Narrator and Philosopher is used partly to assert Meredith's comparative common sense, partly to encompass cold scrutiny of the Pole family while allowing simple acceptance of the heroine, Emilia. Emilia is not analysed: she is presented through physical actions, because she is herself totally unselfconscious and experiences directly through sensation. She has 'the capacity to concentrate all mental and animal vigour into one feeling—this being the power of the soul' (xxvi; 262–3). (The sentence is Mr Pole's observation, with Meredith's interpretation in apposition.) In contrast the Pole girls, to whom everything consists of Fine Shades and Nice Feelings, are remorselessly scrutinised. Meredith sees through them, illuminating what they leave mysterious to themselves. He combats 'fine shades' by the harsh light of peremptory and authoritative exposition. By consigning some of his characters to the purely intellectual scrutiny of the Philosopher while lavishing sympathetic study on his heroine Emilia, Meredith creates a dangerous dichotomy in the structure of his novel and opens himself to charges of sentimentalism—which is his chief object of attack in the novel.

If in *Sandra Belloni* the narrator's presence is too assertive for the reader to feel that he has been permitted an independent understanding of the characters, in *Rhoda Fleming* he is, if anything, too reticent. Rhoda's bullying love of the erring Dahlia, her narrow rigour (which brings about the disastrous forced marriage) are presented with a bland objectivity which misleadingly suggests that the author shares her moralistic code. The novel is an imperfectly controlled early example of the method by which Meredith dramatises the consciousness of a character and leaves the reader to undertake a placing scrutiny. Rhoda is so incapable of realising her unconscious motives that, lacking a forceful narrative presence, Meredith is unable to imply them without falsifying his picture of her personality.

In each of these early novels Meredith evolves a different narrative voice to control the relationship between the characters and the reader. The characterised presence of the narrator persists to some degree throughout his work, but the discussion of literary method in the later novels is related to the characters' intellectual experience. In *The Adventures of Harry Richmond* (1871) he finds a new way forward by allowing narrator and character to coalesce. In this way analysis and action are seen as a continuous expression of personality, and the style of the novel does not have to carry the weight of Meredith's artistic problems.

In *Harry Richmond* he also succeeded for the first time in fusing his delight in epic action and his concern for intense psychological scrutiny. The book appeared after a pause in his career as a novelist—a pause which was largely the result of his pressing need to earn money through journalism after his second marriage in 1864 and the failure of *Vittoria* (1866) to win him popular success. The germ of *Harry Richmond* preceded both *Vittoria* and *Rhoda Fleming*. The novel grew out of a sketch which was to be a 'spanking bid for popularity', and to which Meredith refers in his letters as early as 1861. An outline of some early chapters survives in the Altschul Collection: this had been submitted to Lucas for him to consider serialising the work in *Once a Week*.[11] The outline suggests a romantic extravaganza about a young man, Richmond Roy, and his companion, Contrivance Jack, who is full of schemes for making money in the metropolis. Occasionally we see the germ of the later work:

Chapter 4. *A Terrible Discovery*
(He goes to the great house in the great square, of which he believes his father to be the master, taking Contrivance Jack with him, and discovers that his father is but a visiting singing master there; acting a part)

It is the one mention of a father in the early sketch. (In the final work, Richmond Roy had been a master in Squire Beltham's house years before the story opens.) In the sketch the only relationship shown is the casual companionship and patronage of the young man and Contrivance Jack. The loose, desultory picaresque of the projected story, with its string of adventures following upon one another without accruing significance, is transformed in the final work into a quest for Harry's father which absorbs his childhood. It is a romance more and more stringently tested against the demands of actuality:

> I ceased to live in myself. Through the whole course of lessons, at play-time, in my bed, and round to morning bell, I was hunting my father in an unknown country, generally with the sun setting before me: I ran out of a wood almost into a brook to see it sink as if I had again lost sight of him, and then a sense of darkness brought me back to my natural consciousness, without afflicting me much, but astonishing me. Why was I away from him? (v; 51)

During the long period of gestation the whole conception of the book changed and deepened from picaresque extravaganza to a quest for livable identity.

Another vestigial work which seems to have contributed something to the atmosphere and themes of *Harry Richmond* is the mysterious 'Sir Harry Firebrand of the Beacon or A Knight Errant of the Nineteenth Century'.[12] The title is first mentioned, before 1859, in the Maroon Notebook. In 1887 Meredith mentioned a projected story about 'a Knight of Perfectibility'. And in May 1904, he suggested to H. G. Wells that he should take over the project, entertaining him with a detailed account of the story. These continued references suggest that the book was never written, but (perhaps for this very reason) it seems to have worked in his imagination throughout his career and to have been an element in *Richard Feverel*, *Harry Richmond* and *Beauchamp's Career*. The theme of knight errantry which is so important in *Richard Feverel* derives partly from Meredith's admiration of Cervantes, partly from the imagery of reform current in the mid-nineteenth century.[13] It expressed the central creative perturbation of his career: the relationship of idealism and reality and, linked with this, the contradictory claims of passion and reason. These found expression in his approach to the novel: he attempted to establish a level of reality which would avoid equally the rose pink and the drab, but he frequently found that he could create reality only through alternation, not fusion, of extremes. Perhaps he never wrote the book because the theme was too central to his art for him to work it out through fantasy as he seems to have intended. Again and again in his books, his characters are forced to face the discrepancy between their ideal selves and the consequences which their actions produce in the world. This theme has frequently provided the basis for comedy. Meredith himself cites it in that way in the *Essay on Comedy*; and in many of his works he impels it towards comedy by his adoption of the archaic-literary figure of the knight-errant. But he ranges beyond comedy and shows the disasters that may ensue from too ideal a view of our own potential. In *Harry Richmond* he sets up an antithesis between the world of aspiration and the world of common sense. In the finished novel (which was serialised in the *Cornhill*, September 1870 to November 1871) the aspiring fantasies of growing up are given real form in the external world and romance is tested by the demands of actuality. We are shown the interplay of fantasy and reality in the life of the individual, the need to find connection between prose and poetry. The opposition of the two is expressed in the mutual love and conflict between a father and son: the unteachably alienated grandeur of Richmond Roy whose delusions of regality gain real force in the world by the pressure of his personality, and the wonder-stricken susceptibility of his son, Harry, through whose mouth the story is told—and for whom disillusionment and the discovery of self are intertwined.

Despite its proliferation of incident, its overlapping of a limpid dream-world and confused actuality, the book has at its centre the ordering and clarifying principle of retrospection. It is Meredith's only first person narrative (apart from the unfinished story 'The Gentleman of Fifty and the Damsel of Fifteen' in which alternate chapters are assigned to the two principal characters—whose clashing interpretations show their lack of communication). The problem of the narrator's presence (subjugation of which in *Vittoria* and *Rhoda Fleming* had resulted in incoherences) is here solved by the cohesiveness of the autobiography. At the same time the shifting relationship between father and son allows Meredith to explore the ramified growth of feeling. The two personalities provide the principals of the book's movement: Richmond Roy, explosive, inventive, scintillating, impervious, finally repetitive; Harry Richmond, devious, exploratory, susceptible, seemingly undynamic but growing towards awareness.

Like *Richard Feverel* the book is a *Bildungsroman*. The emotional centre is again the son's need to free himself from an obsessive relationship with his father and so to attain his own identity. Sir Austin was misguided: Richmond Roy is deluded. Fantasy is granted greater significance and warmth in *Harry Richmond*. Whereas Richard's knight-errant aspirations had no validity in the world he inhabited (they waxed ever more grandiose, from saving fallen women to saving Italy from the Austrians), Harry meets and is loved by a real princess. At the same time, it is true that Harry is less altruistic than Richard and the book as a whole less socially concerned. In the earlier book there is a harsh disparity between the gaudy fantasies with which Richard feeds his idealism when separated from Lucy and the true loving world of reality she represented; in *Harry Richmond* we are shown how reality may look like fantasy and fantasy have its own truth. We are never *certain* indeed that Richmond Roy is deluded in his claims to royal birth. In *Harry Richmond* everything (relationships, station, environment) is both shifting and resilient. As a child carried off from his home by his unknown father Harry dreamt that he 'was in a ship of cinnamon-wood upon a sea that rolled mighty, but smooth immense broad waves, and tore thing from thing without a sound or a hurt' (i; 14).[14] The book sustains the buoyancy of that pristine image while showing that for Harry maturity can be reached only by learning to feel the pain of loss.

Hawthorne, in the Preface to *The House of the Seven Gables*, contrasts the Romance and the Novel:

When a writer calls his work a Romance, it need hardly be observed that he wishes to claim a certain latitude, both as to its fashion and material, which he would not have felt himself entitled to assume had he professed to be writing a Novel. The latter form of composition is presumed to aim at a very minute fidelity, not merely to the possible, but to the probable and ordinary course of man's experience. The former—while, as a work of art, it must rigidly subject itself to laws, and while it sins unpardonably so far as it may swerve aside from the truth of the human heart—has fairly a right to present that truth under circumstances, to a great extent, of the writer's own choosing or creation.[15]

In *The Adventures of Harry Richmond* Meredith took the novel as far towards the freedom and self-indulgence of romance as he was ever to go. But although he uses the methods and qualities of romance, its free world is always tested by being set in relationship with detailed psychological representation of the characters to whom the amazing adventures happen. It is his most generous portrayal of the human heart. The world of romance is at once bounded and given a precarious tenure in the world of everyday actuality by being embodied in the figure of Richmond Roy. Seen through his son's eyes, he is at first a towering figure of nobility and splendour who assumes shapes like a god ('I was sure my father was a fountain of gold, and only happened to be travelling', says Harry when his father has not paid his school-bills (v; 64)). Later he is a great actor-comedian, organizing life into masques and pageants; when at last his illusions fail him he seems tragically wrecked, only to reach his apotheosis and destruction in fire at the end of the book. The world of Harry Richmond draws on the same sources of inspiration as *The Shaving of Shagpat*: a world in which dreams become concrete and allegory is expressed in action. Richmond Roy is a victim of Rabesquarat, queen of illusions.

Told briefly the plot sounds like pure romance: Harry Richmond is seized as a child by his father, who is a royal pretender, from the home of his wealthy maternal grandfather, Squire Beltham. He lives with his father in contrasted states of luxury and poverty, is sent off to school, runs away, travels with a gypsy girl (the gypsy sub-plot makes vivid the emotional mingling of freedom and brutality which persists throughout the book). He returns to live with his grandfather, goes in quest of his father, is carried off to Germany by a puritanical ship's captain, rediscovers his father posing as a bronze statue and meets the young Princess Ottilia. He goes to university in Germany, loves and is loved by Ottilia, whom his father is determined he shall marry; he loses her, partly through Richmond Roy's well-meant machinations, and (after manifold adventures) marries his childhood friend and enemy, Janet, who has inherited his grandfather's estate. This apparent farrago of adventures is shifted into significance by being made an image of emerging consciousness.

Meredith told John Morley (*Letters*, i, 204) that he feared he was developing the personality of Harry Richmond too closely for public taste, and to William Hardman he wrote (*Letters*, i, 229) that he was conscious that he had 'carried it so far as to make him perhaps dull towards adolescence and young manhood'. Meredith urged Jessopp not to criticise *Harry Richmond* until he had read the whole.

> Consider first my scheme as a workman. It is to show you the action of minds as well as of fortunes—of here and there men and women vitally animated by their brains at different periods of their lives—and of men and women with something of a look-out upon the world and its destinies;—the mortal ones: the divine I leave to Doctors of D.[16]

The novel's significance is its exploration of a growing identity seeking roots in earth but driven by wind and water, illumined and consumed by fire. The book's imagery constantly solidifies into incident. In this work everything is actual: metaphors take on the form of happenings; aspirations are enacted. In the story of father and son Meredith found the perfect expression of two seemingly contradictory elements in his work: his attraction to the uninhibited possibilities of romance and his powerful consciousness of the inescapable relationship between human actions and their consequences. In the character of Richmond Roy Meredith expresses the reality of fantasy in human life; in the maturing of Harry Richmond he expressed his belief in the necessity of subjugating fantasy to reason. But he responded to the fraught relationship between father and son with a new magnanimity which draws the book constantly towards the warmth and ease of romance despite the process of disillusionment by which Harry comes to maturity. The book's changing method keeps pace with the emerging consciousness of the hero: the double consciousness frequently at work in 'autobiographical' novels, whereby the narrator looks back upon his younger self in judgment and irony, is almost entirely withheld during the account of the hero's boyhood. We are shown everything as it appeared to Harry at the time he experienced it. Meredith presents amazing adventures through the unamazed eyes of childhood. But although the hero's adult judgments are held in abeyance, this does not remove our own adult experience as we read. The child's loving unconsciousness that his father's actions might have more than one meaning creates a poignant tension in the first chapters between what we are told and what we guess. The first chapter, indeed, is presented in the third-person (although the chapter heading reveals that the narrator was the child). There are two descriptions of the visiting stranger:

It was a quiet grey night, and as the doors flew open, a largely-built man, dressed in a high-collared great-coat and fashionable hat of the time, stood clearly defined to view. He carried a light cane, with the point of the silver handle against his under lip. There was nothing formidable in his appearance, and his manner was affectedly affable. He lifted his hat as soon as he found himself face to face with the squire, disclosing a partially bald head, though his whiskering was luxuriant, and a robust condition of manhood was indicated by his erect attitude and the immense swell of his furred great-coat at the chest. His features were exceedingly frank and cheerful. From his superior height, he was enabled to look down quite royally on the man whose repose he had disturbed. (i; 5)

The description mingles sharp observation—the posed gesture of the silver cane against the lower lip, the balding head—with words which enlarge the man's stature: 'erect', 'immense', 'superior height'. He looks down 'quite *royally* on the man *whose repose he had disturbed*' (my italics). Simple description begins to stir with implications: we soon realise that Richmond Roy has disturbed more than Squire Beltham's night's sleep. He has disrupted his life ever since they first met. A few pages later the child is brought downstairs and 'found himself facing the man of the night'.

It appeared to him that the stranger was of enormous size, like the giants of fairy books: for as he stood a little out of the doorway there was a peep of night sky and trees behind him, and the trees looked very much smaller, and hardly any sky was to be seen except over his shoulders. (i; 10)

The child's impression poetically heightens but does not contradict the third-person description. In this way, Meredith convincingly establishes the truth of what he describes and gives us information withheld from the boy: we have an authoritative picture of the enraged grandfather and the devoted West Indian servant Sewis; we hear of the deranged mother. The incident is in itself sufficiently strange and arresting for us to accept the child's own account of the world of the ensuing chapters; it is a partial and intensified but not distorted description of real happenings. The second consciousness can seem to come from the reader not the narrator. And this makes possible a grave, poetic rendering of childhood experience which can encompass the comic without archness.

Harry Richmond writes later in the novel that he has taken trouble to 'shape his style to harmonize with every development of his nature'. It is a technique similar to that of *A Portrait of the Artist as a Young Man* though less thorough-going. Meredith, like Joyce, recognised that the developing personality does not distinguish between ideas and emotions; but the child in this novel grows into the ordinary young man, Harry Richmond, whereas the child in Joyce's *Portrait* grows into the artist. Harry's very ordinariness is shown to be an equilibrium attained with great difficulty out of his unrooted childhood: the poetic qualities of Meredith's novel are most intense, therefore, while Harry is still a child. Not only does Harry have the freshness and energy of any child's vision but he lives in a state of heightened response, because he is prematurely aware of impermanence: he 'was never at peace between any two emotions'. He does not distinguish between emotion and physical environment.

In rain or in sunshine this old farmhouse had a constant resemblance to a wall-flower; and it had the same moist earthy smell, except in the kitchen, where John and Martha Thresher lived, apart from their furniture. (iii; 27)

The structure of the sentences is simple, although it is a simplicity which artfully renders the smooth alien connections of a child's mind: connectives are omitted or string strange clauses together with an easy 'and' or 'but'. When Harry's unseen mother has died

I betrayed the alarming symptom that my imagination was set more on my mother than on my father: I could not help thinking that for any one to go to heaven was stranger than to drive to Dipwell, and I had this idea when my father was clasping me in his arms; but he melted it like snow off the fields. (iii; 33)

Adults effortlessly appear and disappear and the child matter-of-factly accepts events only as they affect him:

By-and-by I lay in a gondola with a young lady. My father made friends fast on our travels: her parents were among the number, and she fell in love with me and enjoyed having the name of Peribanou, which I bestowed on her for her delicious talk of the blue and red-striped posts that would spout up fountains of pearls if they were plucked from their beds, and the palaces that had flown out of the farthest corners of the world, and the city that would some night or other vanish suddenly, leaving bare sea-ripple to say 'Where? where?' as they rolled over. I would have seen her marry my father happily. She was like rest and dreams to me, soft sea and pearls. We entered into an arrangement to correspond for life. Her name was Clara Goodwin; she requested me to go always to the Horse Guards to discover in what part of the world Colonel Goodwin might be serving when I wanted to write to her. I in return could give no permanent address, so I related my history from the beginning. 'To write to you would be the same as writing to a river', she said; and insisted that I should drop the odious name of Roy when I grew a man. My father quarrelled with Colonel Goodwin. (iv; 40–1)

The imperceptible merging of the child's personality into the social world about him begins at school and Meredith gradually increases the commentary of the narrator-Harry as the child grows—but these comments re-live the experience rather than placing it in a scale of values beyond that of the child. The increasing amount of dialogue lessens our subjection to the boy's consciousness, as, with its continuous present and its interplay of points-of-view, it suggests identities other than the central one.

After the half-understood intrigues of school-life (which are recorded in dialogue whose allusions are not understood by the child) Harry is shown as an equal contender in emotional argument with the grandfather to whose care he has returned. Meredith endows him with a trait which he had observed in himself as a young boy and in his own son, Arthur: a heightened power of penetration into what people mean, behind what they say—and a correspondingly inflated sense of omnipotence:[17]

I found that I could see through everybody. Looking at the squire, I thought to myself, 'My father has faults, but he has been cruelly used', [his aunt Dorothy has said this to him] and immediately I forgave the old man; his antipathy to my father seemed a craze, and to account for it I lay in wait for his numerous illogical acts and words, and smiled visibly in contemplation of his rough unreasonable nature, and of my magnanimity. He caught the smile, and interpreted it.

'Grinning at me, Harry; have I made a slip in my grammar, eh?'

Who could feel any further sensitiveness at his fits of irritation, reading him as I did?' (ix; 112)

The laconic account conveys the boy's blindness as well as his insight: Harry speaks of his 'smile'; to his grandfather it looks like a grin. His lofty rhetorical question superbly masks the irritation he feels, while his grandfather's question reveals another real, unmentioned, meaner, source of the boy's irritation with him—his unpolished ways after the courtly father. This new aloofness and power of appraising others does not bring with it awareness of self. When the narrator does begin to comment directly on his own limited understanding of events and to cast his mind forward to the future, the self-conscious intrusion is as much a dramatic presentation of the twenty-one year old's new self-awareness as an objective comment by the still older self. So, he gives set portraits of two women who attract him: Kiomi, the gypsy girl and Mabel Sweetwinter, the miller's daughter, and follows them with slightly grimacing comments:

She was as fresh of her East as the morning when her ancient people struck tents in the track of their shadows. I write of her in the style consonant to my ideas of her at the time.' (xxiii; 261–2)

This was a Saxon beauty in full bud, yellow as mid-May, with the eyes of opening June. Beauty, you will say, is easily painted in that style. But the sort of beauty suits the style, and the well-worn comparisons express the well-known type. Beside Kiomi she was like a rich meadow on the border of the heaths. (xxiii; 263)

These depreciatory remarks on his own style are the start of a more ironic relationship between the older and the younger Harry. The comments of the narrator criticise Harry because he is now capable of self-criticism. He voices feelings of which he was not fully conscious when undergoing them; this suggests that the elements of perception were present in the experience but that he had lacked the courage to focus them. Maturity, the narrative method suggests, consists in the ability to acknowledge and act upon what we always suppressedly know about ourselves. Instead of the intrusive Philosopher intervening to reveal the characters' hidden motives as in *Sandra Belloni*, the narrative method of the book acts out the relationship between experience and scrutiny in the growing identity of the hero:

> The pleasant narrator in the first person is the happy bubbling fool, not the philosopher who has come to know himself and his relations toward the universe. The words of this last are one to twenty; his mind is bent upon the causes of events rather than their progress. As you see me on the page now, I stand somewhere between the two, approximating to the former, but with sufficient of the latter within me to tame the delightful expansiveness proper to that coming hour of marriage-bells and bridal-wreaths. (lvi; 674)

By the end of the book Harry is preparing to abandon 'delightful expansiveness'. Despite the slight air of translation from a German wit by which Meredith represents the labouring consciousness, the style is still graceful and easy when he describes action. The mixed style of the last section represents a coming-together of romance and realism which crowns the book's moral pursuit.

The novel scrutinises various conceptions of romance and shows their relationships to a livable world. In the first part of the book there appears to be a clear contrast between Richmond Roy's world of illusory nobility and the everyday, unimaginative world of Squire Beltham and Janet. At first Richmond Roy is the centre of narrative sympathy; in the later part of the book his theatrical pretensions to nobility are tested against the real loftiness of the princess Ottilia.

She *seems* to be a stock figure from fiction: the heroine of high station who inspires the hero but whom he loses. But although she inhabits the world of a fairy-tale German principality, she is shown to be a young woman whose individuality is animated by intelligence. She is no lay figure to be manipulated by the desires of the hero. Her nobility consists, not in her station, but in the combination of gravely poetic idealism and rationality in her nature. In the central section of the book Harry gradually and unwillingly recognises that the principality is not a fairy-tale kingdom into which he can walk like a conquering folk-hero: it is a small, complex state which exists in the real world and carries real obligations for its inhabitants. Harry charts the growing and shifting relationship between him and Ottilia with an intricacy which rebuffs the caricature boy-meets-Princess story that Richmond Roy is attempting to impose on them. Roy's divorce from reality is shown to include a ruthless disregard for individuality: he responds to types, symbols, plots.

Yet this summary suggests a rigorous moral categorising which in the book is mitigated by the continuity of love between father and son and also by the capaciousness of the book's form. The calm, full realisation of symbol as incident, a kind of imperturbability in the telling of marvels, itself enacts that fusion of reason and poetry which is presented as the highest good. Harry's happiness when he most fully loves Ottilia expresses itself as tranquillity: 'half-stupor, half the folding-in of passion; it was such magical happiness.'

> Not to be awake, yet vividly sensible; to lie calm and reflect, and only to reflect; be satisfied with each succeeding hour and the privations of the hour, and, as if in the depths of a smooth water, to gather fold over patient fold of the submerged self, safe from wounds . . . (xxx; 319)

But the relationship becomes a fiery ordeal of personality for him.

Neither in rank nor in personality is Harry truly a match for Ottilia. She has been brought up to live by reason, a reason which does not exclude passionate emotion but makes it impossible for her to lay her consciousness to sleep. So she needs to be able objectively to believe in the nobility of her lover before she can abandon the duties and princely role for which she has spent her life preparing. Harry is able to adopt a protective attitude towards her when he first meets her as a little girl and as a young invalid which disguises from them both their real inequality. When he meets her again in her own rank and state, the stresses begin. Her lofty ideal of him makes him feel covertly resentful in the midst of his loving admiration. It is the same oppression in love which Meredith had observed earlier in his career in his picture of the relationship between Evan Harrington and Rose. Ottilia, whose closest companion is her tutor, is animated by 'individual, awful *mind*'. And in the version of the novel which persisted till proof (MS, Altschul Collection), Meredith includes a number of long dialogues between Harry and Dr Julius von Karsteg which extend Harry and Ottilia's relationship into a critique of English and German society.[18] German culture at its finest is shown to be capable of a lofty scrutiny of the bases of thought which attains to poetry. Meredith draws on German literature by including set philosophical disquisitions of a type common enough in German fiction but almost unknown in English.[19]

The confusion between 'romance' and 'fiction' is made part of the argument of the novel through the love relationship. Chancellor von Redwitz, obliquely warning Harry against any attempt to win Ottilia by telling him stories of 'romantic' matches, says:

—Young sir, your piece of romance has exaggerated history to caricature. Romances are the destruction of human interest. The moment you begin to move the individuals, they are puppets. 'Nothing but poetry, and I say it who do not read it— . . . nothing but poetry makes romances passable: for poetry is the everlastingly and embracingly human. Without it your fictions are flat foolishness, non-nourishing substance—a species of brandy and gruel!—diet for craving stomachs that can support nothing solider, and must have the weak stuff stiffened.' (xxxiv; 364)

In this novel, the 'everlastingly and embracingly human' is attained with the recognition that another's identity is independent of one's own demands: romance is the desire for omnipotence, the will to make the world and its people approximate to one's vision of them. The attempt to impose our own shape upon the world is seen to be common to beings as contrasted as Richmond Roy and Princess Ottilia. He attempts to make permanent the ephemeral palaces of his pretensions; she demands of Harry an exhausting perfection and cannot love what is fallible in him: 'she was a woman who could only love intelligently—love, that is, in the sense of giving herself' (l; 576). Her disillusionment comes through Richmond Roy's influence upon her destiny: 'the calm oval of her lifted eyelids contemplated him in the fulness of the recognition that this world, of which we hope unuttered things, can be shifted and swayed by an ignis-fatuus' (l; 577). Ottilia's presence in the first half of the book is clear and individual, but once Harry leaves the German kingdom it is made as difficult for us as for Harry to retain a vivid sense of her and she begins to recede into an idealised stereotype, or 'Schöne Seele, and bas bleu' in unsympathetic summary.

Even in the first part of the book there are obscurities and apparent suppressions in her characterisation. Harry seems at times too ready to blame himself for the breakdown of their relationship, in which Ottilia seems to have shown an extreme reserve. This effect is in part due to the revisions which Meredith undertook in proof, knowing that the book was to be serialised. Conscious that he had deliberately made Harry dull in adolescence and young manhood, he recognised that 'Such effects are deadly when appearing in a serial issue' (*Letters*, i, 229). In condensing he cut a scene with Dr Julius von Karsteg, discussions on theology between the English and German tutors, political discussion with the

Prince, and close analysis of Harry's ungenerous impulses. When Meredith revises in manuscript he nearly always amplifies: when he revises in proof he nearly always deletes. His cutting is frequently the result of his distrust of his readers as much as his distrust of his 'Dd. Dd. Dd. uncertain workmanship' (*Letters*, i, 166). In *Beauchamp's Career*, for example, he cut much that seemed to him important because he thought his readers would be dependent on a story.

The most crucial of the sections of *Harry Richmond* to be cut in proof shows that it is Harry's resentful action which keeps him and Ottilia apart after she has told Prince Hermann of her love for Harry. In an unpublished scene (MS 693–706) she waits for him but he avoids her and rides past by a circuitous route: 'pretending to think she meditated and should not be disturbed. I really was near thinking my conduct heroical . . . I see myself cantering!—the sight is unbearable' (MS 693–4). He sees himself transformed into a rigid puppet and in an access of humiliated self-distaste the narrator attempts to account for his action: 'My profound humiliation of late had checked passion's flood. The imps of my nature led me . . .' (MS 697–8). In the manuscript Ottilia assumes that it is noble restraint which leads him to avoid her—he half knows that it is pride. Harry's consciousness of his actual motives makes him sustain the role of the dour laconic Englishman, while feeling more and more resentful that this is forced on him. Ottilia sends him a letter, they meet, and she explains that she has held back so long because she wished to be certain of her own mind. Now she is sure: she wishes him to go into public affairs in England and she hopes to come and see him there. Ottilia is being misled by her dependence on her own free thought and her father's trust in her reason (which gives her apparent freedom of choice while exerting every pressure to make her conform with his views). Harry is sinking under the strain of acting out her ideal of him—which would justify her rationally in the step that emotionally she wants to take. Thus their meeting by night in the library is seen as a last desperate hope for *both* of them in which they step beyond the limits of what they will be able to feel once parted. The histrionic conclusion to the scene where the two middle-aged listeners reveal themselves and Harry's father sets light to the curtains, humiliates the lovers and destroys the particular reality of their feelings by reducing the scene to comedy and stereotype.

By cutting out sections of intellectual discussion and of emotional analysis Meredith makes the published novel rather more conventional in its portrait of the hero. He mitigates the fierce scrutiny of motive. When he later revised the novel he cut several chapters showing the intricate path by which Harry and Janet discover the fullness of their love in the second half of the book. Instead he preserves only the gnomic, summarising passage beginning: 'Is it any waste of time to write of love? The trials of life are in it, but in a narrow ring and a fierier' (lv; 658).

Meredith always avoided the easy convention of sudden changes in relationships and liked to show the stirrings of change within continuity. In the later part of *Harry Richmond* the happenings of the book are preparing Harry for marriage with Ottilia while beneath the surface he is losing hold of his love for her and beginning to turn towards Janet. His images of Ottilia change from rich forest and dawn to dream and shipwreck: 'The image of Ottilia conjured up pictures of a sea of shipwrecks, a scene of immeasurable hopelessness. Still, I strove towards that' (xliv; 511). By the end of the book Janet who had earlier 'caught imagination by the sleeve, and shut it between square whitewashed walls', is 'the fresh English morning'.

The loss of the chapters showing the slow stages by which Janet and Harry are reconciled and move forward into new love, like the loss of the chapters examining the last twists of his relationship to Ottilia before their parting, swings the book a little away from prose reality towards the absolute, the given. The effect shifts away from the difficult acceptance of daily circumstances towards the absolute boon of romance. The book depends more on Richmond Roy and his plotting, less on his son's intricacies.

Harry's major moral preoccupation is with the growth and change of personality, a growth possible to Janet and to him, unheard of for Richmond Roy and impossible to Ottilia—who is idealised in the telling and integrated as a person. An *effect* of change is shown in minor characters like Heriot, the hero at school who is impetuous and unscrupulous in his dealings with women. He is basically unchanged: what made him attractive as a boy makes him unreliable as a man. Harry studies the extent to which he himself has grown—and he has also to convince us of the change in Janet from greedy, demanding child to true and generous woman. The end of the book is equivocal about the extent of change possible to personality—what Harry and Janet experience is an increase of range in their emotional response.

Yet he and Janet had known me longest. Supposing that my idea of myself differed from theirs for the simple reason that I thought of what I had grown to be, and they of what I had been through the previous years? Did I judge by the flower, and they by root and stem? But the flower is a thing of the season; the flower drops off: it may be a different development next year. Did they not therefore judge me soundly? (lvi; 680)

In Harry Richmond himself, Meredith chose as the central consciousness a young man mundane enough in the final balance he achieves, but laid open in heightened and externalised form to the pressures of fantasy and reality, passion and reason, which are an inevitable part of all growth to adulthood. In the figure of Richmond Roy Meredith showed another way of responding to the world, not by growing to 'maturity' but by appropriating the ordinary material of life to a heightened and prolific ego.

The art of the book refuses to choose between them: though it shows the destructiveness of the ego's fantasy, it shows also its bountiful energy. The conditions of the work are generated by the lofty pretensions of Richmond Roy, not by the world of common sense. Its language and imagery are poetic, expressing experience through association. Richmond Roy's constant dramatisation and simplifying elevation of life, together with his son's integral vision while a child, make possible an extraordinary concretion of experience, so that incidents perfectly *are* both symbol and import.

In her discussion of the imagery of *Harry Richmond*, Barbara Hardy rightly suggests that a rigid, dynamic reading of imagery such as that of fire and water in the book runs counter to the flux, momentary crystallisation and disintegration which are typical of the book's movement.[20] The work is intensely mimetic, corresponding to the nature of what is shown rather than imposing a pattern upon it. Richmond Roy's life is, in Keats's phrase, a perpetual allegory. In the most vivid incident, where symbol and happening fuse, Harry rediscovers his father posing as a bronze equestrian statue. The statue represents his employer's princely ancestor. Meredith wrote that he 'resisted every temptation to produce great and startling effects (after the scene of the Statue, which was permissible in art, coming from a boy and coloured by a boy's wonder)' (*Letters*, i, 229). In this scene and, less intensely, throughout the book, Meredith uses a method akin to that of Shakespeare's late comedies: fantastic happenings occur which express deeply secret wishes and fears, while at the same time the characters are realistically presented through the individual speech-styles.

I found the people falling back with amazed exclamations. I—so pre-possessed was I—simply stared at the sudden-flashing white of the statue's eyes. The eyes, from being an instant ago dull carved balls, were animated. They were fixed on me. I was unable to give out a breath. Its chest heaved; both bronze hands struck against the bosom.

'Richmond! my son! Richie! Harry Richmond! Richmond Roy!'

That was what the statue gave forth.

My head was like a ringing pan. I knew it was my father, but my father with death and strangeness, earth, metal, about him; and his voice was like a human cry contending with earth and metal—mine was stifled. I saw him descend. I dismounted. We met at the ropes and embraced. All his figure was stiff, smooth, cold. My arms slid on him. Each time he spoke I thought it an unnatural thing: I myself had not spoken once. (xvi; 197)

Richmond Roy is a man overlaid with heroic trappings: he is a buffoon, yet he possesses the majesty he assumes. He is gleaming, supernatural, a figure for admiration and terror, but he is also imprisoned, hampered and made ridiculous by his accoutrements when he descends from his pedestal. 'Human somewhere, I do believe myself to be. I shall have to be relieved of my shell before I can at all satisfactorily proclaim the fact. I am a human being, believe me' (xvii; 202). His humanity and his rigid image combine in the grandiloquence of his brief address to his son in this passage: all the names mean Harry Richmond, but there are five of them, and the last is the name of both father and son in their role as royal pretenders. He is 'unnatural', unreachable, enclosed in a peculiar reticence which leaves his son dumb and yearning.

The scene conveys that strange universal sense of loss which accompanies longed-for reunion, here heightened until it represents Harry's oppression by his father's personality: 'I became a perfectly mechanical creature.' The laconic, bemused and limpid style renders Harry's impression of the scene. As his father frees himself, Harry takes over the role of frozen statue; his father's extravagant gestures persistently sap the boy's own energy and spontaneity. His response to the scene, his poignant sense of alienation, his fixed gaze at his father's garish scarlet stockings instead of the release of joy in love he has expected—continue to work in his love relationships: when Ottilia's idealisation of him afflicts him with a sense of strain and falsity, he says that she made of him 'a man on a monument'.

Richmond Roy is a man of earth, metal, fire—'a combination of sun and mould'. When Temple and Harry seek him in London in their boyhood they are caught in a fog which gives way to a great fire—a fire which seems to centre on the debtor's prison where Richmond Roy is held (but which is really burning elsewhere). When Harry and Ottilia meet to declare their love and are threatened with disclosure by Baroness Turckems, Richmond Roy appears and uses Ottilia's lamp to set fire to the curtains:

> Me the whole scene affected as if it had burnt my skin. I loathed that picture of him, constantly present to me, of his shivering the glass of Ottilia's semi-classical night-lamp, gravely asking her pardon, and stretching the flame to the curtain, with large eyes blazing on the baroness. The stupid burlesque majesty of it was unendurable to thought. (xxvi; 392–3)

The lamp becomes fire, a fire which is branded on Harry's mind, and begins the chilling of his feelings towards his father. This shift of his emotion is not continuous but fluctuating—it is complicated because he is using the opportunities his father brings him, just as he uses his grandfather's money though he has quarrelled with him. Harry is seeking a self for himself independent of his grandfather's money, his father's suppositious rank, and Ottilia's idealised version of him.

The repetitious, eddying movement of the second part of the book with its account of intrigues and quarrels in parliamentary and fashionable society, is a result of the unteachable nature of Richmond Roy. We know, or seem to know, everything that can be told of him; the reader's interest is held more through the scrutiny of Harry's shifting feelings than through Roy's new tricks for inveigling the Princess Ottilia to England. Sympathy for Harry's change towards his father comes as much through the pace as the matter of the telling. It is the same process by which, earlier, we understood the gradual faltering of the relationship between Harry and Ottilia, dating from the time when he fought a duel with her cousin Otto (in the final draft the duel is described; in the published book it is dismissed). Its unforeseen consequence is what matters; the duel itself is 'A silly business on all sides'.

Just as Richmond Roy embodies the real power of fantasy in human experience, images which occur elsewhere in Meredith's work as emblems of the human condition in this book take on the form of happenings. One such is the image of the subconscious as a mine with the novelist as miner: here, in *Beauchamp's Career* and in *The Amazing Marriage*, the characters' money comes from mines.[21] Repeatedly from *Richard Feverel* to *The Amazing Marriage* Meredith turned back to the idea of the human situation as being like a ship on a stormy sea, with man as captain, pilot, mutinous crew, or mate. Richard Feverel 'had embarked, and was on the waters of life in his own vessel'; Diana goes to Redworth, she says, 'a derelict, bearing a story of the sea; empty of ideas. I remember sailing out of harbour passably well freighted for commerce'. Carinthia, who does not deal in images, cannot suspect her brother's wife, despite all evidence: 'An uncaptained vessel in the winds on high seas was imagined without a picturing of it.' In *Harry Richmond* this image is converted into incident. In *Beauchamp's Career* and *Diana of the Crossways* yachting becomes a proliferating symbol; in *Lord Ormont and his Aminta* swimming expresses sexual discovery and love.

Harry and his friend, Temple, lost in London searching for Richmond Roy, are inveigled aboard the good ship *Priscilla*, which is captained by the whimsical morality-play figure, Captain Welsh. He, convinced that he is rescuing the fifteen-year old boys from liquor and women (a comic misunderstanding which brings the whole episode to the borders of farce), carries them off on a stormy sea-journey to Germany, regaling them with bible-readings on the way. Harry's account of the experience is ruefully amused but underlaid by an awareness that the captain is not merely a grotesque. (Meredith's mixed sympathy and amusement with religious enthusiasts is shown again in the picture of the Salvation Army in *One of Our Conquerors.*) Captain Welsh is an elementally good man, driven by the awful fate of sinners he has loved. The whole incident is at the furthest end of the book's spectrum of improbability, but it is seen through the eyes of adolescent boys and chimes in with their arduous eagerness and intolerance, their search for the right way to behave. As a general metaphor it is related to the whole sweep of the work and it has a precise, if strained, function in the plotting.

At the end of the book Captain Welsh and his ship appear again, this time in a far more directly allegorical manner, as the instruments of retribution. Captain Welsh abducts Lord Edbury, Janet's betrothed, and his mistress, Mabel Sweetwinter, Harry's first love, and absurdly carries them off on a penitential journey. The ship goes down in the North Sea with all aboard, thus conveniently removing the man who was to marry Janet, and making it possible for Harry to regain her. The improbability of this solution would have been acceptable enough in the first part of the book where the barriers between fantasy and reality were laid aside. Here, it jars against the whole structure of what is being shown: against Harry's acceptance of the real world, his own limitations and the limitations of what the world will do for him.

But the reappearance of Captain Welsh at the end of the book also links Harry back to his past. It reminds us of the relationship between root and flower. As Harry says in a passage cut in proof (he is referring to his duel with Prince Otto):

I see that I might have acted wisely & did not; but that is a speculation taken apart from my capabilities. If a man's fate were a forbidden fruit, detached from him, and in front of him, he might hesitate fortunately before plucking it, but, as most of us are aware, the vital half of it lies in the seed-paths we have traversed. We are sons of yesterday, not of the morning, and thereby we may learn that we are not ephemera. The past is our mortal mother, no dead thing. (MS 623, Altschul Collection)

Even more, the reappearance of Captain Welsh and his ship is part of the final resurgence within the book of the older world in which men are driven by extreme ideas and delusions. Captain Welsh is kin to Richmond Roy and to childhood absolutes, not to the chastened, sober Harry. 'My father', says Harry, 'was never insincere in emotion.'

The end of the book reasserts the demonic power of fantasy—and of happenings: fire and shipwrecks, which have been a shifting element in dreams and images throughout the work, now become actual. Shipwreck destroys Harry's rival; fire destroys his ancestral home. 'Fire at the heart, fire at the wings': Riversley Grange is burning. Richmond Roy's splendour is reasserted after his abasement. His exuberant fantasy has planned a great firework display for Janet and Harry at their homecoming from their wedding journey. He goes to his death, generous and futile, trying to save Dorothy, who has always loved him and, disastrously, provided for him. She is not in the house. Instead of Harry and Janet succeeding to the security of Riversley Grange, it burns before their eyes.

They could tell us that the cattle were safe, not a word of my father; and amid shrieks of women at fresh falls of timber and ceiling into the pit of fire, and warnings from the men, we ran the heated circle of the building to find a loophole and offer aid if a living soul should be left; the night around us bright as day, busier than day, and a human now added to elemental horror. Janet would not quit her place. She sent her carriage-horses to Bulsted, and sat in the carriage to see the last of burning Riversley. Each time that I came to her she folded her arms on my neck and kissed me silently.

We gathered from the subsequent testimony of men and women of the household who had collected their wits, that my father must have remained in the doomed old house to look to the safety of my aunt Dorothy. He was never seen again.

THE END

Reality and romance resolve in mythopoeic death. The safe harbourage of Riversley Grange is seen to be as ephemeral as Richmond Roy's majesty. The stout home-counties world is not finally separate from the world of individual fantasy.

3

Beauchamp's Career
Fact and Metaphor: The Establishment of a Style

Beauchamp's Career (1875) is a novel about heroism. It is also a novel about the condition of England in the early eighteen-seventies when the book was being written. It tests a variety of possible heroic attitudes and, while never finally repudiating the concept of heroism, it demonstrates the near-impossibility of finding a significant function for the hero within English Victorian society. Indeed the novel suggests that heroism can now find useful expression only by engaging in the corporate struggle to change society radically. The individualistic quality of heroism may simply be an anachronism. *Beauchamp's Career* is the first full expression of Meredith's intense concern with the life of his times. This aspect of his creative energy reaches its largest range sixteen years later in *One of Our Conquerors*. The complex irony of *Beauchamp's Career*, and later, *The Tragic Comedians*, depends on recognition of their exact historical concerns as well as of the extent to which Meredith distances them from topicality.

Meredith told Gissing:

> You may have histories, but you cannot have novels on periods of long ago. A novel can only reflect the moods of men and women around us, and after all, in depicting the present we are dealing with the past, because the one is enfolded in the other.[1]

Meredith was keenly interested in the intellectual and critical ideas of his contemporaries although he always avoided committing himself positively to any organised body of opinion. Politically, he appeared to be in sympathy with liberal rationalism, particularly the liberal nucleus centred in Morley's *Fortnightly Review*, in which *Beauchamp's Career* was serialised (August 1874–December 1875). But the cast of his mind was at once too sceptical and too emotional to accept rationalism as a broad enough basis for political action and temperamentally he regretted liberalism's lack of 'cohesion' and 'vital principle'.[2]

Repeatedly in Meredith's work an intellectual debate is dramatised and dissipated through the events of the book. By this means he shows the mutation undergone by ideas in action. Current critical debates frequently provide not only the context of Meredith's art as a novelist but the actual theme of the book; he reproduces the complexity of debate without trying to provide a resolution. One can already see this equivocal form in *Richard Feverel*, with its testing of the moral implications of evolutionary theory, and it is still present in his last book, *The Amazing Marriage*, where the novel debates—and uses—the possibilities of both psychological realism and romance. *Beauchamp's Career* studies the political temper of Meredith's day; it is radical in tendency but works through the medium of ideas rather than action. It is not, like the earlier condition-of-England novels, concerned to expose practical abuses but rather to analyse the psychological disablements of society. There is even something ultimately evasive about the laconic melodrama of the book's conclusion. To put it more positively: the novel diagnoses society's diseases; it does not pretend that they can be healed by the novelist's art. The equivocal relationship between history and fiction is felt as a psychical and social problem rooted in the England of the time, not simply a technical one to be solved by the novelist.

The mood of the work is peculiarly sober, intellectual, acute. It offers none of the free solutions, the liberated antics of *Harry Richmond*, which immediately preceded it.

Whereas earlier the world of illusions was, in a sense, substantiated in the person of Richmond Roy, in *Beauchamp's Career* society seems impervious even to the characters' reasonable hopes and aspirations. The novel itself is obsessively preoccupied with the checks, the gaps, between consciousness and expression. It is a novel in which all the characters are weighed down with the responsibilities of intelligent adult life.

In his letters Meredith described the novel as 'an attempt to show the forces round a young man at the present day, in England, who would move them, and finds them unutterably solid' (i, 242). The unutterably solid forces are the forces of reaction; they are implicit in the nature of any society, grounded, inevitably, in habit and custom. The sections on French society show that this is not a peculiarly English problem, but the 'insular commonplaces' of English society are felt to be as solid and irremovable as the geographical fact that England is an island. England is the hero and the villain of Beauchamp's life:

> he loved his country, and for another and a broader love, growing out of his first passion, fought it; and being small by comparison, and finding no giant of the Philistines disposed to receive a stone in his foreskull, pummelled the obmutescent mass, to the confusion of a conceivable epic. His indifferent England refused it to him. (iv; 39–40)

Frustration, shapelessness of experience, the impossibility of translating complex perceptions into anything other than crass emblematic actions: these problems are central to the book's meaning. They are also problems in the design of the work.

Beauchamp is in love with the future because that is the world of ideas, in which ideals can flower. But the future is also, dangerously, a dream generated out of the individual's inner life, not part of that physically present world we hold in common. Meredith, like his protagonist, finding himself isolated, was tempted to appeal to the future over the heads of his contemporaries. Radicals, comments the narrator, seek to lift 'our clay soil on a lever of Archimedes'.

> They have perchance a foot of our earth, and perpetually do they seem to be producing an effect, perpetually does the whole land roll back on them. You have not surely to be reminded that it hurts them; the weight is immense. (xxvii; 293)

'The weight is immense': the wit of this comment, which shifts metaphor back into substance, goes to the heart of Beauchamp's dilemma. How can new theories generate the energy to shift the mass of human beings? The relationship between the ideal world of fiction and the recalcitrance of fact engaged Meredith's artistry with special power at this period in his career. It is a theme which is worked out again in *The Tragic Comedians* and *Diana of the Crossways*.

Beauchamp's Career opens a new stage in Meredith's own career. The change is marked both in structure and style. In some ways his artistic problems run parallel to Beauchamp's political problems. He described the book as 'philosophical-political with no powerful stream of adventure'. Towards the end of the novel, as the story enters its final, entirely painful sequence of loss and death, Meredith speaks out, distorting the water imagery which has run through the entire book. His apologia measures and bridges the distance between the buoyant central section of the book and the foreboding which now begins to darken the close. He speaks of his inability to create a mystery. (Then, typically, at the end of this rather self-pitying apology he offers an account of Rosamund's feelings in pregnancy which creates mystery not through twists of plot but through scrupulous analysis.)

> My way is like a Rhone island in the summer drought, stony, unattractive and difficult between the two forceful streams of the unreal and the over-real, which delight mankind—honour to the conjurors! My people conquer nothing, win none; they are actual, yet uncommon. It is the clock-work of the brain that they are directed to set in

motion, and—poor troop of actors to vacant benches!—the conscience residing in thoughtfulness which they would appeal to; and if you are there impervious to them, we are lost: back I go to my wilderness, where, as you perceive, I have contracted the habit of listening to my own voice more than is good. (xlviii; 552–3)

Meredith's art finds its value only within a world of ideas, but the significance of the ideas depends upon their perceived connection with actual life. 'Idealism is an atmosphere, whose effects of grandeur are wrought out through a series of illusions, that are illusions to the sense within us only when divorced from the groundwork of the real' (*Letters*, i, 156). Richmond Roy's ideals were illusory because enclosed in the fantasy-world of his prodigious ego; those of Beauchamp and Dr Shrapnel—and Meredith—are never in this novel utterly 'divorced from the groundwork of the real'. Idealism in this novel is seen at its most extreme in Dr Shrapnel who claims that 'The flesh *is* a dream. The soul only is life'. But the work itself also shows the power of the dreaming flesh.

Meredith himself here eschews romance, tragedy, the epic, all those satisfying ideal moulds into which experience may be set, in order to show his people in this novel tussling with the undynamic complexities of intelligent life. The novel even eschews prophecy, outside the epistle of Dr Shrapnel, though a sense of half-perceived human possibilities is allowed to trouble almost all the characters, even the least imaginative. But neither is Meredith satisfied with what he would call the 'over-real': the method of describing and judging life through objects and appetites. (Because Beauchamp eats a good breakfast of farm produce brought to London from his uncle's estate, Rosamund Culling cynically imagines him to be a half-hearted lover and 'a politician less alarming in practice than in theory': we are not invited to agree.)

The novel's title registers the contrary impulses at work in the protagonist. 'Career' suggests both a sober progress towards personal professional achievement and the wild flight of a horseman unable to control his beast. Beauchamp's worldly career suffers constant reverses: he leaves the navy where he seemed certain to gain advancement when he meets Dr Shrapnel and dedicates himself to political action; he fails to win a parliamentary seat because of his dash to France at the height of the campaign in answer to the cryptic summons of Renée, his first love; he loses the hand of Cecilia, the Conservative heiress who loves him—who has become in some ways more radical than he and whose wealth would have made his enterprise of a Radical newspaper possible—because through a mixture of motives he delays too long. He does win the love and respect of Dr Shrapnel, of the poor, of the women who surround him; his uncle Romfrey does finally apologise to Dr Shrapnel for the unjustified horse-whipping he has given him.

'He hasn't marched on London with a couple of hundred thousand men: no, he hasn't done that', the earl said, glancing back in his mind through Beauchamp's career. 'And he escapes what Stukely calls his nation's scourge, in the shape of a statue turned out by an English chisel. No: we haven't had much public excitement out of him. But one thing he did do: *he got me down on my knees!*' (lv; 616)

The italics are Romfrey's. Rosamund feels the bitter humour of the situation: 'the immense deal thought of it by the earl, and the very little that Nevil would think of it'.

Moreover, Meredith here demonstrates how tangled the motives for action are. Romfrey was ready to believe that Shrapnel had insulted Rosamund Culling, because he was angry that Shrapnel had taken over Beauchamp, because Shrapnel had provided the means for the defence of a poacher on Romfrey's land, and, particularly, because Romfrey himself was conscious of the equivocal position in which Rosamund Culling stood as his housekeeper. He was finally brought to apologise by Rosamund's insistence after their marriage, while she was pregnant with a possible heir to the old man. Rosamund had married the earl in large measure out of concern for his relationship with her beloved Beauchamp. Though Beauchamp is at the centre of the book, Meredith emphasises constantly that he is not the centre of the world. Neither is he a picaresque hero free to move on to the next adventure, the next woman, sloughing off old selves and old companions. All the other characters have equivalent continuous centres of self whose demands are as urgent and engrossing as Beauchamp's own.

In the last section Beauchamp achieves a happy, rational marriage to Jenny Denham, Shrapnel's niece. He dies, leaving her with a young breast-fed baby, when he attempts to rescue two small working-class boys from drowning. One drowns with him, one he saves. Throughout the book Beauchamp has sought a way out of enclosed self. When the moment comes for selfless action he meets it. But the moment's significance is blurred and limited. Beauchamp's career is in some ways the inverse of that other sailor hero, Lord Jim. Jim misses his high heroic moment and survives to become for a time the leader of a people who need him. Beauchamp, who is concerned with broad social change, responds to the moment, saves the single working-class child and thereby wipes out all that his sustained political endeavours might have brought about. Personal heroism has no bearing on social change; it is meaningful only on its own intense but limited terms. The final image of the book is sour and bleak. The two old men, Shrapnel, the radical who hoped to see Beauchamp carry on his ideas, and Romfrey, the conservative whose own baby recently died, 'alive one hour in his arms', so that Beauchamp was his blood heir, watch the dragging of the river for Beauchamp's body.

> 'My lord! my lord!' sobbed the woman, and dropped on her knees.
>
> 'What's this?' the earl said, drawing his hand away from the woman's clutch at it.
>
> 'She's the mother, my lord', several explained to him.

'Mother of what?'

'My boy', the woman cried, and dragged the urchin to Lord Romfrey's feet, cleaning her boy's face with her apron.

'It's the boy Commander Beauchamp drowned to save', said a man.

All the lights of the ring were turned on the head of the boy. Dr Shrapnel's eyes and Lord Romfrey's fell on the abashed little creature. The boy struck out both arms to get his fists against his eyelids.

This is what we have in exchange for Beauchamp!

It was not uttered, but it was visible in the blank stare at one another of the two men who loved Beauchamp, after they had examined the insignificant bit of mudbank life remaining in this world in the place of him.

THE END

The cruelty of this ending casts an unremitting light on the way love for an individual will override all other sympathies and opinions. The small boy saved is an affront to both old men.

Because the novel is so concerned with the relationship between personal and political life and between dream and fact it becomes, by an intelligent and unexpected extension, preoccupied with metaphor: the characters as well as the novelist explore the insights and distortions created by metaphor and the whole relationship between rhetoric and actuality, language and action, becomes crucial to the book's meaning. In *Beauchamp's Career* Meredith is not exploring dream country for its own sake, as to some extent he was in *Harry Richmond*. He is fixedly occupied with actualities. But he recognises that actuality—the present day—harbours both individual isolated dreams and also national nightmares. We can see these perceptions affecting the factual background to the novel, the new control of lyrical language and the organising metaphors of the work.

Henry James objected to Meredith's failure to place his stories in a specific place and time.[3] In *Beauchamp's Career* Meredith places his period as exactly as he was ever to do. He draws on his experiences of campaigning for Maxse in the Southampton election of 1868; the initial impulse of Beauchamp and his career obviously derives from the strenuous debate which Meredith and Maxse carried on in their letters during the sixties.[4] Many of the characters in the electioneering chapters are drawn from actual persons. More important is the way in which Meredith's whole relationship with Maxse helped to form his own political views and his perceptions about the temperamental sources of political attitudes. In their correspondence Meredith constantly tempers Maxse's absolutes with wry sympathetic perceptions; many of the topics they discuss are taken up in *Beauchamp's Career*: conscription; vegetarianism; suffrage; christianity; prayer; baptism; co-operative labour. Maxse was a type of the hero to Meredith—not the less because the latter sometimes pointed out the absurdities of his friend's position. He was a guileless fanatic, a Don Quixote in love with the future, obsessed with ideas and possibilities. He gave complex human form to a type which fascinated Meredith because it was essential to the working of his fiction: the man passionately addicted to ideas, who has 'drunk the questioning cup'.

Meredith's principal characters live 'in the idea'; they are fanatical in emotion, in their views, in their will. They have to be, to carry the novel's freight of ideas. Maxse is wrought into the fantasy of the 'Knight Errant of the Nineteenth Century' which I have already discussed in its bearing on Harry Richmond. 'Sir Harry Firebrand of the Beacon' is a fantasy type derived from Maxse by a Peacockian abstraction. Shrapnel is 'a fire-worshipper'; Beauchamp is a 'firebrand,' will 'make a bonfire of himself' and 'has a rocket-brain' according to the practical Tory, Tuckham. Sir Harry Firebrand, as Meredith once playfully addresses Maxse, is the incendiary radical, but also a forerunner of the 'man immensely rich, imbued with Herbert Spencer's ideas, full of the all-importance of the future and its problems, always dwelling in them, always working on them' who 'has a scheme . . . for moving the earth'. So Meredith described him in his account of 'The Knight Errant of the Nineteenth Century', a fantasy plot which he offered in 1904 to H. G. Wells.[5] The fact that radicalism is linked in Meredith's mind with knight-errantry and fantasy suggests both his attraction and mistrust. In life, unlike Beauchamp, Maxse survived his own radicalism to become a high Tory Admiral, married to a wife called Cecilia.

In *Beauchamp's Career* Meredith avoids fantasy by pinning the book closely into history. He gave Maxse some advice as to how to read Carlyle and Carlyle is a crucial presence in the novel. Carlyle, he told Maxse, is 'a humourist'. 'Swim on his pages, take his poetry and fine grisly laughter, his manliness, together with some splendid teaching. . . . I don't agree with Carlyle a bit, but I do enjoy him' (*Letters*, i, 174). And later he writes: 'Spiritual light he has to illuminate a nation. Of practical little or none, and he beats his own brains out with emphasis' (i, 200). Both these passages were written at the time Meredith was working on *Beauchamp's Career*. A much later comment suggests that he felt a kinship between his own type of stylistic achievement and that of Carlyle.

He was the greatest of the Britons of his time—and after the British fashion of not coming near perfection; Titanic, not Olympian: a heaver of rocks, not a shaper. But if he did no perfect work, he had lightning's power to strike out marvellous pictures and reach to the inmost of men with a phrase. (*Letters*, ii, 333)

At one level it may be that the novel is a response to Carlyle's earlier injunction to him to write history:

The story is that Mrs Carlyle begged Carlyle to read 'Richard Feverel'. He did so, and said, 'Ma dear, that young man's nae fule. Ask him here'. When he came, as Meredith himself told me, he talked long with him on deep things, and begged him to come often. He said, 'Man, ye suld write heestory! Ye hae a heestorian in ye!' Meredith replied that novel-writing was his way of writing history,

> but Carlyle would not quite accept that. He did not argue about it, but rather doubted over it, as if there were more in it than he had thought at first.[6]

John W. Morris reads the book as a straightforward tribute from Meredith to Carlyle.[7] 'In effect, Meredith reports himself in *Beauchamp's Career* as having accepted Carlyle's advice to write history, reserving only the right to keep his characters at blood heat.' Morris points out the ways in which Beauchamp corresponds to the Carlylean hero: he is an aristocrat leading the people, he puts love of country above self. But this interpretation misses the two-edged nature of Carlyle's role in the book. His representative within the book is Dr Shrapnel: this in itself suggests limits to Meredith's tribute. Dr Shrapnel never escapes from the shadow of Don Quixote. Dr Shrapnel's style is described by the wise intellectual, Seymour Austin, as 'the puffing of a giant: a strong wind rather than speech . . . men who labour to force their dreams on mankind and turn vapour into fact, usually adopt such a style'. Like Carlyle, Shrapnel seems to be a spiritual, not a practical guide. Beauchamp's firing to intellectual life comes as a result of reading Carlyle.

> His favourite author was one writing of Heroes, in (so she esteemed it) a style resembling either early architecture or utter dilapidation, so loose and rough it seemed; a wind-in-the-orchard style, that tumbled down here and there an appreciable fruit with uncouth bluster; sentences without commencements running to abrupt endings and smoke, like waves against a sea-wall, learned dictionary words giving a hand to street-slang, and accents falling on them haphazard, like slant rays from driving clouds; all the pages in a breeze, the whole book producing a kind of electrical agitation in the mind and the joints. This was its effect on the lady. To her the incomprehensible was the abominable, for she had our country's high critical feeling; but he, while admitting that he could not quite master it, liked it. (ii; 22)

The characterisation of Carlyle's style (which recreates it in the way that Pater's prose does a picture) and Rosamund's prosaic reactions to it suggest Meredith's aesthetic kinship with its obscurities. ('Concerning style, thought is tough, and dealing with thought produces toughness. Or when strong emotion is in tide against the active mind, there is perforce confusion'. So Meredith justified his method to Baker.) Carlyle is venerated as a spiritual guide—a prophetic presence—'the nearest to being an inspired writer of any man in our time', Meredith told Maxse. But he is not a practical guide: 'when he would apply his eminent spiritual wisdom to the course of legislation, he is no more sagacious nor useful nor temperate than a flash of lightning in a grocer's shop' (*Letters*, i, 200). Carlyle, then, has a range of conflicting roles within the artistry of the novel: he offers Meredith a parallel for his own problems in persuading an English audience to listen to what he is saying; he focusses the problem of history and fiction which is implicit in the work as a whole; he is personated in Dr Shrapnel; and, most important, his book *Heroes and Hero-Worship* illuminates Beauchamp intellectually.

Meredith's use of tutelary books in this novel differs in one basic and suggestive way from the rest of his work. Elsewhere the books themselves are fictitious: in *Richard Feverel*, for instance, he used Diaper Sandoe's volume of verse and Sir Austin's 'Pilgrim's Scrip'; in *Diana of the Crossways* we have Diaries and Memoirs describing her and her own novels which form an unconscious commentary on her life; in *One of Our Conquerors* he presents *The Rajah in London* (London, Limbo and Sons, 1889), 'a Poem or Dramatic Satire', through which he offers a longer perspective on the oddities of British society, and Colney Durance's serial tale 'The Rival Tongues', which creates an absurd fantasy-parallel to the problems of language and inarticulateness explored psychologically within the book. In *The Amazing Marriage* Carinthia is guided by her dead father's book of aphorisms, 'Maxims for Men'. This idiosyncratic device intensifies the cerebral effect of his novels; his people live not only in a world of ideas but of books and writing.

Much of the material for these fictitious books comes from Meredith's own unpublished notebooks. But in *Beauchamp's Career* the books are real, available to the reader as well as to Beauchamp. *Heroes and Hero-Worship*, Ruskin's *The Stones of Venice*, Byron, Dante, Plato (Beauchamp's last enthusiasm), all are part of the open intellectual world in which we move. There is nothing fanciful about them; their oppositions are the oppositions inherent in cultural history.

Three models for the hero are offered within the book. The Byronic hero is set against the Carlylean hero. Hovering unexorcised behind them is the presence of Don Quixote. The Byronic hero represents the archaic selfhood implicit in heroism. In the opening pages of chapter four, which Meredith inserted at Morley's suggestion as a kind of explanation and apology for his hero and his artistic method, he states: '"Beauchampism" is the obverse of Byronism, and rarely woos your sympathy, shuns the statuesque pathetic, or any kind of posturing' (iv; 38). The book opens with young Nevil Beauchamp's nearest approach to the absurdities of heroism—the despatch of a personal challenge in stilted French to the officers of the Imperial Guard because England has been insulted. He never receives a reply.

Throughout the novel he is tested by being set in Byronic situations and tempted to respond with the swagger and panache and daring which would win him approval in his own class. Renée, his French love, reads Byron and it is in relation to Renée that Beauchamp is most often tempted to revert to the Byronic mode of heroism. Before her arranged marriage to the Count, Beauchamp attempts to persuade her to continue at sea with him, flying off with her like a corsair. When she summons him to France he barely avoids duelling with 'the handsomest young man in France' and he is still ready to carry her off from her loveless marriage. Under Dr Shrapnel's tutelage his view of women as beings to be protected and won but not argued with or treated as equals gradually changes, so that when Renée flees from her husband to him in London he cannot accept the life she would entail:

'But we must live in England', he cried abruptly out of his inner mind.

'Oh! not England, Italy, Italy!' Renée exclaimed: 'Italy, or Greece: anywhere where we have sunlight.' (xl; 454)

Nevil is committed to England, both its reality and his dream of what it might be. The novel is another document in that debate about nationality and race, about patriotism, which so fascinated the eighteen-seventies and which found its most profound expression in *Daniel Deronda*. England, the island kingdom, permeates the novel's argument and imagery. Its place in the metaphorical structure can best be dealt with later in this discussion. The hyper-consciousness of England's intactness and of the threat of invasion in the novel probably derives from a particular, previously unrecognised source which makes sense of the book's opening, focusses its meaning for the eighteen-seventies and illuminates some of the political peculiarities of Beauchamp's position, such as his militant foreign policy.

In May 1871 *Blackwood's Magazine* published an extraordinary article called 'The Battle of Dorking'.[8] This was a masterly fictional forecast of the invasion of England by the Prussians. Even now Chesney's fictitious first person account, written supposedly 'fifty years after' the heroic but hopeless stand of the inexperienced volunteer army and the take-over of the country by German soldiers, reads with chilling authority. (It was actually published in translation in Berlin in 1940 as propaganda. *Was England Erwartet. Voraussagen eines englischen Militärschriftstellers aus dem Jahre 1871*.) The article was quickly republished as a pamphlet and ran into seven editions. The defeat of France by the Prussians in 1870 had made it clear that England was by no means immune from attack. Her navy was crucial to her defence since her one great natural advantage was that of being an island.

The story caused the utmost consternation, even panic, throughout the country. I. F. Clarke gives a full account of its reception in his article 'The Battle of Dorking, 1871–1914' and he points out that four months after the appearance of the story Gladstone warned the country against its alarmism in a speech at the Working Men's Liberal Association at Whitby.[9] The venue was appropriate. For Chesney was not simply conjuring up military terrors. He was concerned to expose the social conditions which led to England's unpreparedness. He attacked the complacency of the middle-classes, the greed of the rich, and the failure to understand that England's prosperity was based on being a 'workshop'.

Fools that we were! We thought that all this wealth and prosperity were sent to us by Providence, and could not stop coming! In our blindness we did not see that we were merely a big workshop, making up the things which came from all parts of the world.

This 'Providential' view was seen also in the rising birth-rate and in the illusion of limitless prosperity which the growing Empire provided: 'in those days young men could be sent out to India, or into the army and navy'. Something of the attitude Chesney was attacking is expressed in the novel by Romfrey, who believes in the Empire, in games rather than military service as a training, and in the impregnable defence of the sea.

And he was not one of those who do penance for that sweating indolence in the fits of desperate panic. Beauchamp's argument that the rich idler begets the idling vagabond, the rich wagerer the brutal swindler, the general thirst for a mad round of recreation a generally-increasing disposition to avoid serious work, and the unbraced moral tone of the country an indifference to national responsibility . . . Mr Romfrey laughed at scornfully, affirming that our manufactures could take care of themselves. As for invasion, we are circled by the sea.

Providence has done that for us, and may be relied on to do more in an emergency. (xxxiii; 369)

Chesney made the point that England's prosperity was unsound because the workers could not share the fruits of their labours. Gerard Manley Hopkins wrote in his journal for 6 August 1871 that 'The Battle of Dorking and the fear of revolution make me sad now'. The entry came a few days after his well known letter to Bridges (2 August) in which he spoke of 'the Communist future'.

It is what Carlyle has long threatened and foretold. But his writings are, as he might himself say, 'most inefficacious-strenuous heaven-protestations, caterwaul, and Cassandra-wailings'. Some years ago when he published his *Shooting Niagara* he did make some practical suggestions but so vague that they should rather be called 'too dubious moonstone-grindings and on the whole impracticable-practical unveracities'. However, I am afraid some great revolution is not far off. Horrible to say, in a manner I am a Communist.

Strikingly, Carlyle and 'The Battle of Dorking' had projected Gerard Manley Hopkins, too, into new visions of the future. Like Hopkins, Meredith responded to the radical implications of the short story—which was not in itself at all a radical document. Beauchamp recognises that to be a sailor defending his country from attack does not go to the source of her difficulties (although his foreign policy is surprisingly militant for a Radical). He prefers to work as a civilian within society to change it at its roots.

Chesney's account of the coming battle would have had one special significance for Meredith. The central battle of the account takes place outside Dorking. Meredith's cottage at Box Hill was just above the town and the battleground described was actually the countryside he could see from his house. Indeed his house lay in the troops' path and would have been among those blown up. In the opening chapter of *Beauchamp's Career* it is a French invasion that is threatened but Meredith's heightened rhetoric reproduces as well as mocks the fevered atmosphere of national crisis generated in 1871 by what, after all, was a work of pure fiction.

The Press creates 'Panic'—Meredith makes 'Panic' a personified image of hysteria: 'once fairly awakened, she directed a stare toward the terrific foreign contortionists, and became in an instant all stormy nightcap and fingers starving for the bell-rope' (i; 3). The rumoured soldiers 'wore wide red breeches blown out by Fame, big as her cheeks, and a ten thousand of that sort would never think of retreating'.

> Then, lest [Panic] should have been taken too seriously, the Press, which had kindled, proceeded to extinguish her with the formidable engines called leading articles, which fling fire or water, as the occasion may require. It turned out that we had ships ready for launching, and certain regiments coming home from India; hedges we had, and a spirited body of yeomanry; and we had pluck and patriotism, the father and mother of volunteers innumerable. Things were not so bad. (i; 3)

These were the answers given at the time to the fictional forecast in 'The Battle of Dorking'.

With a sudden shift of tone ('Similes are very well in their way') Meredith changes from the mock-heroic, mock military and journalistic style in which he has been working. He had, after all, been a leader writer himself in the past. He offers an account of what he is attempting in his work: 'I must try to paint for you what is, not that which I imagine'.

> This day, this hour, this life, and even politics, the centre and throbbing heart of it (enough, when unburlesqued, to blow the down off the gossamer-stump of fiction at a single breath, I have heard tell), must be treated of: men, and the ideas of men, which are . . . actually the motives of men in greater degree than their appetites: these are my theme . . . (i; 6–7)

The tone is still slightly equivocal. He has 'heard tell' that politics will blow the down off fiction. It is not clear how far he believes it.

Meredith had been irritated by Maxse's demand in 1871

that 'in these serious times' he 'take to political writing'. 'I am to be allowed to produce one vol. novels on Questions of the Day' (*Letters*, i, 233). The effect of 'The Battle of Dorking' had brought home to the English the *power* of fiction. Fears and dreams generate reality in such a way that outer and inner life cannot safely be distinguished; fiction can actually become a part of history. These are perceptions which Meredith had already explored through a different pattern in *Harry Richmond*. Now he applied them to the nature of modern society. The concept of heroism, which combines ideal and event, becomes the key to an exploration of personality in society and to the stresses within society's view of itself.[10] He attempts to penetrate more directly than through 'Questions of the Day' into the covert *assumptions* of English society in the seventies.

Heroism traditionally expresses itself in action—the actions of battle, of triumphant love, of revenge, of rescue. Each of these concepts of heroism is tested within the book and each turns out to have only a momentary relevance to the human situation. The 'old stable ego' finds its highest expression in the concept of heroism: the 'hero' is beyond change. Yet heroism tends to take the form of extreme acts which thrust the personality far outside the expected circle of behaviour. Through this paradox in the idea of heroism Meredith explores the interplay between society's ideal and the life of the individual and—moving into more exacting novelistic territory—the relationship between what a man existentially is, in each moment as it passes, and what he conceptually is, when imagined, epitomised, by himself and others.

Beauchamp never aspires to be a hero; he recognises heroism in others, and the distance he travels can be measured by the shift from his youthful enthusiasm for military exploits to his recognition of Shrapnel's heroic quality: 'The dedication of a man's life and whole mind to a cause, there's heroism' (xxxiii; 358). It is in the nature of Radicalism that it offers no present prizes: no 'praise and rewards'. 'Radicals, always marching to the triumph, never taste it; and for Tories it is Dead Sea fruit, ashes in their mouths!' (xxvii; 294). Beauchamp has been brought up in a code which closely links personal prowess with personal honour. He struggles to free himself from the habits of thought of his class, but he cannot range far outside the gentlemanly code. Much of his energy in the novel is engrossed by his campaign to force his Uncle to apologise to Dr Shrapnel. Beauchamp is both an individual and a type—at odds with his times and the past and yet a product of them. This must be the dilemma of any radical and Meredith makes him bear the weight of his period: 'I think his History a picture of the time—taking its mental action, and material ease and indifference, to be a necessary element of the picture' (*Letters*, i, 243).

The 'condition of England' is a psychical as well as a social condition. For this reason much of the book's political thought is expressed through personal relationships. Beauchamp's spiritual and emotional development towards the future—towards true radicalism—is tracked through his changing attitude to women. Beauchamp is attracted first to Renée, the gentle, sensual French girl, because he can play out the traditional masculine role towards her: protect her, condescend to her, worship her. He loses Cecilia finally because he cannot understand that she is growing independently of him through the force of her passionate love for him. He is unconscious of her passion. He comes to her for peace, seeing her always and only as an ideal upper-class English woman: cool, peaceful, a princess. He never reaches to that centre of herself which is turbulent, 'radicalish' and argumentative.

The psychological portraiture of Cecilia is one of the most radical achievements in the novel. She is in an agony of thought which can rarely reach expression. Her dilemma serves as a commentary on society: society admires her for her perfect behaviour; gradually she comes to see that her inhibiting desire to please, to be perfect, is a form of self-worship. She breaks into the energetic world of ideas and adopts them with delirious completeness. Her vegetarianism is an expression of her passion for Beauchamp: 'she saw the innocent pasturing beasts, she saw the act of slaughter'. The separation between men and women, the way in which women are excluded from discussion in conservative society, is brought home in the scene where Cecilia and Mrs Lespel penetrate into the deserted smoking room to tear down posters libelling Beauchamp. They have never been in there before. 'A strange air to breathe, was it not?', says Mrs Lespel, whose house it is. 'The less men and women know of one another, the happier for them' (xx; 208).

Beauchamp grows beyond this view. He develops beyond 'that element of the barbarous which went largely to form his emotional nature', which 'enjoys wresting a woman from the enemy and subduing her personally'. He claims early in the book 'There may be women who think as well as feel. I don't know them'. He ends by marrying the new thinking woman, dowerless Jenny. Her comment, 'Does incessant battling keep the intellect clear?', sets him on the last stage of his spiritual journey away from the assertion of self. She is the daughter of a poet, foster daughter of Dr Shrapnel. Jenny, though, is no visionary. She champions good sense, she is independent in thought and feeling but far less radical in her views than either Beauchamp or Shrapnel. Indeed, she is less radical than Cecilia is by the end of the novel. She and Beauchamp make a marriage of affection which *represents* equality between the sexes but never gives vivid life to it. All that is most truly radical in Meredith's own apprehension of women is expressed in the psychological portrait of Cecilia's growth and in the failure of the relationship between her and Beauchamp.

Beauchamp reaches out past the Byronic, the conservative, in his relationships. He is never put to the test of an extended marriage. The book is concerned with courtship—with the future, with potentiality. It was only in the eighteen-eighties that Meredith turned to the married situation. Beauchamp is a successor to that last lecture in *Heroes and Hero-Worship*: 'The Hero as King. Cromwell, Napoleon: Modern Revolutionism'. His is to be the modern type of the hero, but the process of the book indicates that modern heroism can have no personal centre. It can exist only through relationships, through arguments, even perhaps through inaction.

The language through which Meredith attempts to suggest the nature of Beauchamp's achievement shows a crucial uncertainty in the writer's own mind: he never solves the problem of escaping from the archaic language concepts of his subject. Rosamund—to whom he gives many of the book's perceptions for which he cannot find form in anything but traditional intuitive utterance—thinks of Beauchamp just before his marriage to Jenny: the scene reveals, through stream-of-consciousness, Rosamund's secretly acknowledged love for Beauchamp as she draws near labour. Her 'embracing imagination' 'revealed him to her as one who had other than failed: rather as one in mid career, in mid forest, who, by force of character, advancing in self-conquest, strikes his impress right and left around him, because of his aim at stars' (lvi; 617). The language of romance, of errant knights, the imprecision of 'strikes his impress right and left . . . because of his aim at stars' may be justified as part of Rosamund's thought patterns, but the sonorities of this language, the solemn parallelisms and brief phrases coalescing upon the word 'strikes' show the difficulties of adapting a ritualised figure like that of the hero into a modern, complicated, argumentative man committed to the welfare of society, not maidens in distress. It is the problem of the characters in the book, but it is also to some extent a problem which Meredith shares.

In a number of senses *Beauchamp's Career* is a novel

about the limits of imagination. In order technically to express this theme Meredith explores lyrical language with a new awareness and control. He registers the division between the expressive inner processes of personality and the checks and inhibitions which prevent them from finding an equivalent living complexity in either speech or action. Although his method is to concentrate on the inner processes of personality he senses that actions may be a more intense expression of personality than sentiments can be: 'Our deathlessness is in what we do, not in what we are' because 'a human act once set in motion flows on forever'. Though the narrator in *Beauchamp's Career* might not entirely agree with that narrative comment in *Rhoda Fleming* he continues to feel the disparity between motive and consequence as the source of both comedy and tragedy. The ability to accept the unforeseen consequences of our actions is the basis of his morality. He also sees that the consequences of action may reveal hidden motives more surely than action itself. ('The wishes we secretly nurse are the fathers of our future' (Maroon Notebook).) He recurs frequently to the image of the 'two men' within us: our ideal self lives in motives, our existential self in action.

Action, in all Meredith's novels, is simplification and this is particularly so in *Beauchamp's Career*. The complexity of motives is momentarily resolved—the consequences have not yet begun. Action becomes stasis: a point of rest. He frequently by-passes any account of the act itself, allowing us to know of it only retrospectively by observing its consequences (as with Romfrey's horse-whipping of Shrapnel). And in big scenes of confrontation and performance he frequently moves into another narrative key: at such moments he uses the language of melodrama, which is itself a convention of simplification. It was no accident, for instance, that Sandra, the heroine of the two earlier novels, written when he was first beset by the problems of close analysis and heroic perspective, was an opera-singer. *Sandra Belloni* was 'without a climax of incident (finis waving no nuptial torch)—the climax being all in a development of character—' (*Letters*, i, 140), but Meredith there created an effect of completed pattern by appropriating operatic conventions. He gathered all the characters, on their various pursuits, into a wood for the concluding *tutti*.[11]

Writing to an American admirer in 1887, Meredith commented:

> You say that there are few scenes. Is it so throughout? My method has been to prepare my readers for a crucial exhibition of the personae, and then to give the scene in the fullest of their blood and brain under stress of a fiery situation. (*Letters*, ii, 398)

Meredith exploits the novel's correspondence to life, which rarely refines itself into 'scenes' and flows on continuously. At the same time he involves the reader in shifting intimacies with diverse characters. No fixed distance is maintained: at one moment a character may be presented as caricature, at the next with full psychological realism. A 'scene' of vital importance may be passed over laconically or obliquely referred to by a character who has played a minor role in it, while at other times the intricacies of a single consciousness expand to macrocosmic proportions. The different paces of telling imply evaluation, but not necessarily Meredith's own evaluation. Sometimes the brevity of an episode suggests the characters' own limited awareness of its importance; sometimes the episode's place in the total structure of the book makes its importance clear. The laconic presentation of Beauchamp's death makes us share the shock felt by the characters within the book and leaves us to create its significance for ourselves. But sometimes the effect is less successful: we are left with a sense of issues bypassed, emotional necessities unrealised. Renée's flight from her husband to Beauchamp is veiled discreetly by allusion instead of being dramatized. We are given insufficient information to follow imaginatively the intricacies of Beauchamp's moral choice. His decision to persuade her to return to France may thus seem merely self-protective.

Meredith frequently witholds information until a much later point in the story. We are used to discovering the details of a situation piecemeal in life; within the novels the disarranged sequence of discovery works as an image of intrigue, search, secrecy and the necessity of suspending judgment. It also distances us from the characters: in some ways we know far more than they, in others less. Meredith's allusive presentation of information is in part naturalistic but is also akin to dream. It opens the novel out towards romance and poetry, in which information is supplied, not in logical sequence, but according to the moment's necessity. As Ralph Freedman expresses it in *The Lyrical Novel*: 'Lyrical immediacy is different from the immediacy of narrative action as we find it, for example, in the battle scenes of *War and Peace*. It is an immediacy of portraiture, an availability of themes and motifs to the reader's glance without the interposition of a narrative world.'[12] This immediacy of portraiture is well analysed in Ramon Fernandez' account of Meredith's style: 'all valid knowledge of life is the reflection upon man in the moment wherein he acts'; 'the point of consciousness was the relation of individuals' characters to their acts, and his analysis consisted in his becoming conscious of his dramatic intuition of things'. Intelligence is indispensable not only for full *comprehension*, but for full *realisation* of life. Lucidity makes possible a more fully lived, because more fully apprehended, life.

Fernandez perceives the interpenetration between imagery and analysis which is so essential to Meredith's work: images 'constitute a defense system against abstraction', they 'verify the analysis' and 'succeed in preserving what is specific in a moment of sensibility'. Repeatedly, what seems at first only florid and obscure shifts into clear insight as the reader *realises* fully the image presented.[13]

The realisation involves the reader not simply in an interpretative role but in a creative act. It is not enough for him to accept the narrative account; it is not enough even to live through the consciousnesses of the characters; he must remake the author's metaphors as well as act them out. This makes for strenuous pleasure: one sees what Joyce admired in Meredith. The problem is that the poetic intensity of reading demanded may exhaust the reader and ultimately dull his sensibility.

In *Beauchamp's Career* we are shown the waking of diverse characters to imaginative life. Metaphor, which is never quite the same as consciousness, mediates the experience for us as readers. It allows us to enact it. In Meredith's use of metaphor the densely imagistic flow of a character's thought can become another person's inner life alive within us. Yet the characters within the novel are deeply distrustful of metaphor. For some it implies too vital an imaginative life—something barely under control and out of scale with the 'insular commonplaces' of English society. Rosamund, for example, values propriety, in part because of her own equivocal position; she likes 'composed simplicity' because it does not rouse her hidden hysterical terrors. She is so deeply offended by the tone and style of Dr Shrapnel's speech when she visits him that she allows Romfrey to gain the impression that he has in some way scandalised her, even physically assaulted her. The account of her reaction to Shrapnel's speech makes it clear that she dreads images because her own imagination is untutored and uncontrolled:

> It was perceptible to her that a species of mad metaphor had been wriggling and tearing its passage through a thorn-bush in his discourse, with the furious urgency of a sheep in a panic; but where the ostensible subject ended and the metaphor commenced, and which was which at the conclusion, she found it difficult to discern. (xii; 121)

Her inner life is densely figurative but her speech is coolly laconic: this discrepancy is felt in most of the characters in the novel. Their inner fervours can find no social expression and so, in a sense, none of the controls of communication. This forces them to extreme acts which can form an emblem for their intense inner drives. Action becomes a form of metaphor.

Beauchamp himself is irritated by metaphor because he has little concern with niceties of tone. He lacks the 'light and easy semi-irony' which Cecilia likes. He is always in earnest, always taking things literally, wanting practical guides to conduct:

> Where lay *his* weakness? [thinks Cecilia] Evidently in the belief that he had thought profoundly. But what minor item of insufficiency or feebleness was discernible? She discovered that he could be easily fretted by similes and metaphors: they set him staggering and groping like an ancient knight of faëry in a forest bewitched. (xvi; 159)

Again, there comes a shift into metaphor to describe the *effect* of metaphor and once more Beauchamp is linked with the anachronistic romance imagery which makes him seem less dangerous and more appealing to the women around him. But in this passage the metaphor is less directly and clearly an offshoot of Cecilia's thought-style. It seems to be set in that imagistic area between the character and the narrator's consciousness which is the frequent alternative to direct narrative assertion in Meredith's work. Metaphor creates an effect of objectivity because the reader participates in its creation, but its terms covertly control our field of vision. Cecilia distrusts metaphor because she feels that it is used by men to exclude women from the world of abstract ideas. (Her own most admired author is Dante.) In conversation on conservatism and liberalism with her intellectual guide Seymour Austin, she objects to his image for liberalism:

> 'Liberalism stakes too much on the chance of gain. It is uncomfortably seated on half-a-dozen horses; and it has to feed them too, and on varieties of corn.'
>
> 'Yes', Miss Halkett said, pausing, 'and I know you would not talk

down to me, but the use of imagery makes me feel that I am addressed as a primitive intelligence.'

'That's the fault of my trying at condensation, as the hieroglyphists put an animal for a paragraph.' (xxviii; 300)

Seymour Austin's apology is in part Meredith's own.

In *The Art of Authorship* George Bainton quotes a letter which Meredith sent in reply to a request for guidance to young writers:

I have no style, though I suppose my work is distinctive. I am too experimental in phrases to be other than a misleading guide. I can say that I have never written without having clear in vision the thing put to paper; and yet this has been the cause of roughness and uncommonness in the form of speech.[14]

Meredith goes on to suggest that the best early training for a prose writer is poetry: the 'Addisonian style can run only in the bounds of a brook, it cannot be largely allusive or guardedly imaginative.' In *Celt and Saxon* he remarks that 'Fervidness is the core of style' and it is clear that in *Beauchamp's Career* he is determined to register the range of personality through a condensed poetic style—a style demanding constant imaginative response from the reader and capable of rendering the changes in sensibility which may never find issue in any one clear action. But he intersperses this with dialogue which is extraordinarily naturalistic, catching the ellipses of familiar speech with no attempt to smooth or generalise them. He is also interested in the differing *attitudes* to language of the various political parties. Beauchamp claims that 'Tory arguments always come to epithets' and Cecil Baskelett, the most mean-spirited of Tories, likes to feel his superiority to others by fixing them in a phrase. Rosamund to him is, with sly intent, 'Mistress Culling', Beauchamp's social concern is 'Humanitomtity'. He reduces the enthusiastic poetry of Shrapnel's letter to absurdity as he reads it aloud. His own speech style makes the heroic ludicrous, the mysterious flatly comprehensible:

he has 'the art of stripping his fellow-man and so posturing him as to make every movement of the comical wretch puppet-like, constrained, stiff, and foolish' (xi; 98). He is the cynic who shies away from imaginative possibilities and veils his timidity with urbane malice.

Captain Baskelett had undertaken to skip, and was murmuring in sing-song some of the phrases that warned him off: '"History—Bible of Humanity; ... Permanency—enthusiast's dream—despot's aim—clutch of dead men's fingers in live flesh ... Man animal; man angel; man rooted; man winged" ... Really, all this is too bad.' (xxix; 322)

Baskelett is presented as a particularly English type—the reductive satirist. He represents that self-satisfied repudiation of experiment, idealism and imagination which Meredith saw as the most repressive quality of English society.[15] Meredith interpreted hostile criticism of his own style as part of that pattern. He follows an imagistic description of Renée's photograph with this truculent apology:

The writer in this country will, however, be made safest, and the excellent body of self-appointed thongmen, who walk up and down our ranks flapping their leathern straps to terrorize us from experiments in imagery, will best be satisfied, by the statement that she was indescribable: a term that exacts no labour of mind from him or from them, for it flows off the pen as readily as it fills a vacuum. (xxxiv; 382)

The tone is unpleasant; Meredith has here allowed himself to be goaded into aggressive display. There is, certainly, a strong element of exhibitionism in Meredith's method. Metaphors 'civilise' us, as he claims in *Diana*, because they enable us to understand levels of our being which would otherwise remain inchoate and beyond the reach of reason. But metaphor also strongly suggests the presence of a creator and Meredith frequently uses it in order to suggest simultaneously the views of an observer and a character. The control implicit in formulating metaphor presupposes the author, and there is a besetting danger that a brilliant metaphor will reflect light on his presence instead of illuminating the situation he describes. In Meredith's work, as in a James novel, even when the author is concealed he is expressively present in the idiosyncratic style. The style of each writer shows us him in the process of evaluating experience: James through hesitations, circumlocutions and assertions, Meredith through epigrams and imagery.

Metaphor in Meredith's novels links consciousness and the unconscious, outer action and the fantasy life within. It can direct our response to a character or action without the novelist needing to provide reasons for our judgment. It is often organic, arising out of the characters and revealing levels of which they themselves are unconscious. It may counter our emotional response to the particular moment, or provide us with a way of foreseeing actions from the moment they are engendered in the characters. Always, Meredith's principal purpose is to intensify our consciousness and register his own. When he attains simplicity he does so by resolving a prismatic cluster of associations into a clearly focussed image, which yet retains its rainbow splay of meaning. Any passage of Meredith's prose reveals how essential metaphor was to him. Even in the *Essay on Comedy*, it is through metaphor and allusion, through description and suggestion, that his account of comedy is presented.

Henry James, contrasting Meredith's lyricism with the work of the quintessential novelist Balzac, describes him as 'that bright particular genius of our own day, George Meredith, who so strikes us as hitching winged horses to the chariot of his prose—steeds who prance and dance and caracole, who strain the traces, attempt to quit the ground, and yearn for the upper air'.[16] Meredith, in James's view, runs counter to the peculiar strengths of the novel by using methods so closely akin to those of poetry: the methods of compression, ellipsis, suggestion and metaphorical association. Virginia Woolf, comparing him with the Russian novelists, puts it thus:

They accumulate: they accept ugliness: they seek to understand; they penetrate further and further into the human soul with their terrible power of sustained insight and their undeviating reverence for truth. But Meredith takes truth by storm; he takes it with a phrase, and his best phrases are not mere phrases but are compact of many different observations, fused into one, and flashed out in a line of brilliant light.

And discussing his method of description she says: 'That is the way, as one trusts at such moments, that the art of fiction will develop.'[17]

Meredith himself saw his prose and his poetry as twin expressions of his purpose and expressed surprise that Trevelyan had attempted to discuss them separately.[18] Typically his manner in the novels is condensed and associative, close to much poetry and close also to unstructured thought-processes. This is the particular advantage of the style as a means of recording personality.

Everard Romfrey is the most imaginatively hidebound of the characters in *Beauchamp's Career*. Yet Meredith expresses Romfrey's distress at the time of Beauchamp's illness and delirium through a series of grotesque images:

he became aware of the monotony of a tuneless chant, as if, it struck him, an insane young chorister or canon were galloping straight on end hippomaniacally through the Psalms. (l; 570)

it reminded him of a string of winter geese changeing waters.

The voice of a broomstick-witch in the clouds could not be thinner and stranger: Lord Romfrey had some such thought. (l; 571)

The phrase 'Lord Romfrey had some such thought' indicates Meredith's uneasiness at assigning images to him. He resolves this by combining the role of Romfrey and narrator as the scene proceeds:

He thought the poor thing on the bed must be going, resolving to a cry, unwinding itself violently in its hurricane of speech, that was not speech nor exclamation, rather the tongue let loose to run to the death. It seemed to be out in mid-sea, up wave and down wave. (l; 573)

The extraordinary imagistic condensation of this passage

renders both the watcher's emotional response and the physical experience of delirium through thronging, half-rendered images of extremity, dissolution, the rope running out of control, the animal hunted 'to the death'—all held within the over-riding image of a ship weltering in a gale.

All the earlier images, apart from the fanciful witch's broomstick, are related to Romfrey's habitual experience (that of a hunting country squire) which is heightened into new consciousness. The last passage quoted invokes Beauchamp's experience as a sailor: Meredith expresses simultaneously the delirium as both Romfrey and Beauchamp undergo it.

Romfrey is placed in a situation which takes him beyond his stock language and stock responses; before coming he had 'described to his wife Nevil's chattering of hundreds to the minute. He had not realized the description, which had been only his manner of painting delirium'. The experience forces him to 'realize the description' and, opened to realization, he is forced also for the first time to recognise Dr Shrapnel as a suffering man instead of an ogre.

To indicate Romfrey's expanding imaginative grasp Meredith assigns imagery to him. In the next chapter he shows Romfrey's power to abandon imagery and face the fact itself (shortly after the passage quoted below, the images become absolute in a marvellously vivid and moving dream of desolation).

> The delirious voice haunted him. It came no longer accompanied by images and likenesses to this and that of animate nature, which were relieving and distracting; it came to him in its mortal nakedness—an afflicting incessant ringing peal, bare as death's ribs in telling of death. (li; 578)

The last phrase of this passage is an example of Meredith's own inherently metaphorical thought and expression. Dramatically, the reference to 'death's ribs' weakens his observation of Romfrey confronting the unadorned fact; its syntactical relationship to the rest of the sentence suggests that it is the author's amplification rather than Romfrey's own.

Meredith's failing is the opposite of Romfrey's. He cannot resist 'realizing' images and resuscitating dead metaphors even when they confuse his main observation. His world of thought is inveterately animated and all words spawn images. His comment to Bainton, quoted above, shows that he knows it.

In the most consciously experimental of his earlier novels, *Sandra Belloni*, he includes within the fabric of the novel much discussion and criticism of his methods through the figure of the Philosopher and through dramatised argument. After a series of technical experiments by Meredith in presenting the action, Purcell Barrett and Cornelia discuss the style of a story written by Tracy Runningbrook (a figure based on Swinburne as Meredithian novelist).

> You say, 'He coins words'; and he certainly forces the phrase here and there, I must admit. The point to be considered is, whether fiction demands a perfectly smooth surface. Undoubtedly a scientific work does, and a philosophical treatise should. When we ask for facts simply, we feel the intrusion of a style. Of fiction it is part. (viii; 63)

Purcell continues with the pronouncement that the English, though more imaginative than most races, are unpractised in imagination because of the Puritan element 'in literature as elsewhere'. He follows this with a consideration of the relationship between poetry and prose in English as opposed to French.

> Our language is not rich in subtleties for prose. A writer who is not servile and has insight, must coin from his own mint. In poetry we are rich enough; but in prose also we owe everything to the licence our poets have taken in the teeth of critics. Shall I give you examples? It is not necessary. Our simplest prose style is nearer to poetry with us, for this reason, that the poets have made it. Read French poetry. With the first couplet the sails are full, and you have left the shores of prose

far behind. Mr Runningbrook coins words and risks expressions because an imaginative Englishman, pen in hand, is the cadet and vagabond of the family—an exploring adventurer; whereas to a Frenchman it all comes inherited like a well filled purse. (viii; 64)

Purcell clearly speaks for Meredith here and what he says continues to be relevant to Meredith's use of language in the novel. Purcell says that in English, poetry is the central creative mode of the language; the prose-writer is driven to experiment by the search for subtlety in prose. The novelist is seeking a prose language equivalent in intensity to poetry. For Meredith such language could be discovered only by approximating prose to poetic method. He sought to combine the compression of poetry with the complete statement of prose. This sometimes leads him to write like the 'hieroglyphist who put an animal instead of a paragraph'.[19]

In *Beauchamp's Career* his style is first fully established. Meredith increasingly recognised the artistic dangers of metaphor and of a highly conscious and ornate style, though he never repudiated either: 'There's nothing like a metaphor for an evasion', comments Beauchamp.[20] At this stage in his career he still hopes that full communication may be possible; the characters' isolation from each other is seen as the result of social conditions which may be changed. He has not yet sounded the depths of his characters' tragic inarticulateness as he was to do in his only other fully social novel, *One of Our Conquerors*.

For a novel with a Radical hero *Beauchamp's Career* gives very little place to the poor: a vignette of a poor man's cottage, a group waiting for news at the crisis of Beauchamp's illness, a passing reference to a poacher, the mother of the boy Beauchamp saved. Yet it is a more genuinely radical novel than, for example, *Felix Holt the Radical*, because it is concerned with transforming the sensibility not only of its characters but of its readers. *Felix Holt*'s conclusion is quietist. Its use of the detective form creates an artistic effect of solution though the political issues raised in the book are not settled, or even carefully argued.

Throughout his work one sees how Meredith deliberately avoids any settled plot structure. Conventional plot is, in his view, an invitation to conservatism: once having recognised the pattern we are as readers absolved from active responsibility. Instead, the book pursues the vagaries of personality and shows the continuity between emotional relationships and political and imaginative growth. Outside character sustained metaphors provide the ordering principle of the work.

The prose style of any novel must suggest the quality of the author's relationship to his characters and, by extension, to the world at large. In *Beauchamp's Career* Meredith also implies standards for judgment through two structural metaphors. He uses the sea as an organic metaphor, whose significance shifts as the book grows. Instead of acting as a control, which gives a moral focus defined and imposed by the author, this kind of metaphor becomes part of the ambience of experience; it helps us to participate more richly in it. But Meredith also uses a more 'directive' extended metaphor: that of knight errantry. The chivalric imagery in the novel is invoked partly for its anachronistic effect. It represents an impulse which is noble and yet preposterous when seen in relation to present-day English society. The gentlemanly ideal is the last decadent form of chivalry which can now recognise heroism only in military actions and personal 'honour'; Beauchamp himself is affected by this ideal and must struggle to regenerate England without the tools of a new vocabulary —or only such as he can glean from his reading of Carlyle and his mentor Dr Shrapnel. Beauchamp's unharnessed idealistic energy is constantly seeking an appropriate form and as constantly failing to find it. Although he is a radical he cannot easily slough off the gentlemanly rituals: in particular, his dogged and disproportionate insistence that his uncle offer Dr Shrapnel a formal apology derives from a dying world of chivalry and knits the chivalric imagery into the action. His growth towards maturity can to some extent be charted by his move away from traditional chivalry: he will not fight a duel with Renée's would-be lover; he will not give up his political prospects to save Renée when she flees to him in London, although she has come in answer to his earlier assurance that he will remain always ready to receive her; he is not abashed by the recognition that Cecilia's fortune would save him from his money difficulties and allow him to open *The Dawn*, his projected Radical newspaper; he marries Jenny Denham knowing that love will grow between them out of companionship of feeling and ideas, not as the result of any overwhelming passion.

Chivalry dramatises events and emotions: this highlights the close kinship between heroism and egoism. But the other 'hero' in the book, Dr Shrapnel, has gone utterly beyond self in his commitment to ideals. He lives for the future and so to a great extent lives in his imagination. This concentration on imaginative vision, often at the expense of practical life, endows him with Quixotic dignity. Meredith emphasises his physical likeness to Don Quixote: his immense height and thinness, his outlandish garb, his imperturbability. When he is pelted with bags of flour at the election the description shifts from his absurd appearance to an effect of authoritative dignity: 'The popular cry proclaimed him a ghost, and he walked like one, impassive, blanched, and silent' (xxvii; 295). His selfhood is sublimated into his energetic Carlylean prose, through which he seeks to change the world into that world of the future which he already inhabits in his radical visions. His dreams are not archaic or exclusive of fact: they are simply painfully difficult to realise without a total reshaping of society. He offers gnomic prophecy, not a programme of reform.

It is Beauchamp who is to give practical form to his ideas. Towards the end of the book, after Beauchamp's marriage, there is already a suggestion that the engrossing compromises of family life are beginning to deflect Beauchamp from the long-sustained commitment essential to bring about reform. The acceptance of the need for compromise is Beauchamp's final shift away from the archaic chivalric world—but it is also seen as a move away from social idealism. Beauchamp's nature is two-sided: the quixotic and the reasonable man are at war. After an apparent victory for reason in his marriage to Jenny his life is finally defined by a personal heroic action, terribly limited in its effect but pure in its completeness.

For this final scene the imagery of chivalry does not need to be invoked because it is confirmed by the action. The chivalric imagery—in which I include the 'Firebrand' references and the 'romance' images of the passages analysed earlier—is always related to the narrator's point-of-view. It has the effect of 'placing' Beauchamp, often ironically, while at the same time it reinforces his heroic status even when his behaviour is equivocal. It evades certain problems of definition by creating an ironic historical perspective for the concept of 'heroism'. It distances us as readers from the experience of the characters in the novel. It is itself a fiction.

The sea, unlike knight-errantry, is part of the world of fact on which the novel is founded. Britain is an island surrounded by the sea. But the sea is not limited to a single historical meaning. *Beauchamp's Career* is a novel of politics. Yet none of the crucial *actions* of the characters derives directly from political principle. The narrative incidents are deliberately and often painfully inadequate as a dramatisation of the complex emotional pressures which produce them. So the characters' individual thought processes, inner metaphors, habitual speech modes, carry the flux of the book's meaning. The significance of feelings below the level of consciousness is frequently expressed through sea imagery and through the actual recurrent presence of the sea in the novel. The sea reminds us that life cannot all be totally contained by rationalism.

The sea is constantly used as a setting for episodes in the book. Beauchamp is in the navy and we hear from a distance of his acts of heroism when he takes command of an anti-slavery cutter. The one moment of freedom for Renée and Beauchamp comes when they sail all night upon the Adriatic and see the dawn rise over the Alps. (Renée is usually associated with inland waters, canals and rivers, whereas Cecilia loves yachts and sailing.) Beauchamp's courtship of and marriage to Jenny happens during a long sea cruise. The action of the novel takes place on the Sussex coast. Beauchamp dies in the estuary.

But the sea flows through the action in other ways: there is a strong consciousness of the two shores of England and France, separated by brief but stormy water, which Beauchamp crosses to reach Renée and which she in turn must cross when she runs away from her husband to him. The ebb and flow of the tide is related to the movement of the courtship between Beauchamp and Cecilia: 'he had swayed her on ebb and flood so long'. After her engagement to the solid Blackburn Tuckham, Cecilia (in one of the most psychologically complex and moving sequences in the story) acknowledges to herself her love for Beauchamp as, chill and passive, she sails round the coast on a pleasure trip. 'The revelling libertine open sea wedded her to Beauchamp in that veiled cold spiritual manner she could muse on as a circumstance out of her life' (xlviii; 550). At the end of the book, as Beauchamp's enormous ideals and ambitions dwindle or founder, the imagery of mud-flats and shallow water becomes insistent. Beauchamp drowns saving a 'bit of mud bank life'. Beauchamp's prowess as a sailor and yachtsman is an image for his inner aspirations: he is an adventurer, voyager, free-thinker, in contrast to the tenacious, game-preserving, landed Romfrey. England is an island surrounded by tides and storms and this comes to represent the aristocrats' fear of the people. 'The poor are everlastingly, unrelievedly, in the abysses of the great sea', yet they are also, in Tuckham's Tory view, the storms and winds which threaten the settled land of society. Romfrey places his trust in the encircling sea when it comes to foreign policy. For the privileged, with their schooners and yachts, who can set off for France or Italy at a whim, the sea is simply a cultural passage way.

Yet the sea is to be dreaded even by characters like Cecilia and her imagery of distress is almost always expressed through the sea: Beauchamp's wife, she feels despairingly, would have to be 'rooted in nothing, in sea-water'. She feels herself like a 'weed of the sea' as she lies upstairs in bed knowing that below her her father and Nevil are contesting possession of her: 'the assurance in her mind that neither of them would give ground . . . dragged her this way and that till she swayed lifeless between them . . . To love is to be on the sea, out of sight of land' (xxxv; 394).

The sea is not simply *used* imagistically in the novel but *acknowledged* as a natural force. It reminds the reader of the uncontrollable world surrounding characters and reader and able to annihilate them and their ideas. In his choice of narrative metaphor Meredith suggested a profound challenge to that easy rationalism common to the liberal reader who would first have read the book as it was serialised in *The Fortnightly Review*. It was a challenge to Morley and Maxse, and in a different way to Meredith himself as he struggled to reconcile reason and the unconscious through his art.

4

The Egoist
The Two Masks and the Idea of Comedy

THROUGHOUT his work Meredith draws attention to his use of the modes of comedy and tragedy and insists on their interpenetration. The effectiveness of the novel as a form lies in large measure in its power to mingle the comic and tragic and to demonstrate to us the inextricably mixed quality of life. As Meredith said in the *Essay on Comedy*: 'Life we know too well is not a comedy, but something strangely mixed. Nor is comedy a vile mask'.[1] Meredith's mastery of high comedy, with its surface tension of words remaining smooth above the forceful currents of man's animal nature, has led some critics to treat him as essentially a precious writer, an ironist in the tradition of his father-in-law, Peacock, in whose work men exist only as the sum total of their views. None of Meredith's books however offers an impervious comic completeness: even *Evan Harrington*, the most self-satisfied of them, includes the painful exploration of the psychology of the dying cripple girl, Julie Bonner. In his portrait of Juliana, conventionally a sentimental figure, Meredith probes her feelings with an astringency and truth which operates outside the pattern of comedy. What he shows about her (her jealousy, her frustration, her meanness, her eagerness to be loved) is not easily appealing—its justification is its psychological probity. Its propriety comes from its truth to life outside the novel, not from artistic patterns within the work.

A writer with so powerful a belief in individual identity and free-will might well be expected to find the sustaining of a single mode particularly unattractive ('But I do not make a plot. If my characters, as I have them at heart, before I begin on them, were boxed in a plot, they would soon lose the lines of their features.')[2] The gratification we are permitted is rarely that of the perfect cadence; it is rather a sense of the new range of possibility discovered by modulation. Meredith's belief in the individual's responsibility for his fate is an element in this attitude. Plot conventions are akin to fatalism: once the reader has recognised the pattern he is absolved from responsibility—this may be true also of the characters, who in their suffering are passive instruments of something preordained. When Meredith takes a traditional story, such as the happy marriage against odds in *Richard Feverel*, he subjects it to fierce pressures instead of allowing it to be its own justification.

Meredith attempts to combine the free flow of experience with scenes which probe and epitomise personality under stress. Mrs Mountstuart in *The Egoist* (1879) says 'I suppose there are clever people who do see deep into the breast while dialogue is in progress. One reads of them.' Despite his concern for what is 'deep in the breast', Meredith recognises that analysis and action tend to be disjoined in human behaviour: we recognise ourselves and others *in retrospect*. He tries to demonstrate this through the form of his novels and he shows in the body of the work how far this disjunction is the spring of comedy and of tragedy. The notebooks and portfolio jottings frequently comment on the idea:

The first point in studying others is to be disengaged from ourselves.
The book of our common humanity lies in our own bosoms
To know ourselves is more a matter of will than of insight.
(Blue notebook: all on one page)

Three ways of looking on men—either with the personal eye, or with the philosophic mind, or with the inward mirror which reflects them as it were in a personal framework:—this last the safest for action
(Aristophanes Portfolio)

I come to the conclusion that the wisdom of men is greater than their courage. They know more than they dare own that they know.

(Dramatic Dialogue Portfolio)

Meredith did not have the integral vision needed to sustain and fulfil tragedy in the novel. George Eliot's stable concern for her characters allows her to use the novel as a tragic form. Hardy's indeflectible calm, which makes coincidence part of a larger determinism, could not be encompassed by Meredith's febrile and kaleidoscopic method. Meredith's relationship to his characters works by appropriation and rejection, so that he moves between lyricism and irony. The tragic episodes in his novels are the appalled reversal of comedy. Equally, 'humour in its intense strain has a seat somewhere about the mouth of tragedy, giving it the enigmatical faint wry pull at a corner visible at times upon the dreadful mask' (*Celt and Saxon* (vi; 57)). Richard Feverel goes to his death in a duel, abandoning his wife and child, because the woman who seduced him writes that Lord Mountfalcon has attempted to seduce his wife. Beauchamp loses his life in a heroic act, 'an insignificant bit of mudbank life remaining in this world in the place of him'. Alvan, in *The Tragic Comedians* (1880), makes tragedy inevitable by handing Clotilde back to her mother with a theatrical smile instead of recognising that her flight to him has used up the last ounce of her courage.

The tragic hero who stalks the books is Othello: a man bereft and fooled, ruined by something akin to the comedy of errors in which characters not only lack self-knowledge but also crucial information.[3] In *The Tragic Comedians* Meredith overtly uses the parallels between his hero and Othello: the special pain of both works comes from the reader's knowledge and impotence. Meredith responded to Othello's personality and situation as to an idealised version of his own character and early experience. In his approach to tragedy there is always a sense of the radical concurrence of comedy and tragedy.

The 'Dramatic Dialogue' Portfolio includes a list of *Tragic Tales* which suggest a Corneille-like view of tragedy as the conflict between public and private good. For example: 'Felman—the Polish leader. His son Sigismund deemed guilty of betraying the cause. Count Felman sentences him to death.' The tales represent Meredith's admiration for the epic, but the neo-classical idea of tragedy does not operate in the novels themselves.

The late *One of Our Conquerors* (1891) is the novel closest to sustained tragedy. The hero is ruined and elevated by suffering—but here again Meredith uses the *methods* of comedy for his tragic purposes. In his youth Victor Radnor has married an elderly widow, Mrs Burman, and run away with her young companion, Nataly. Their love is faithfully sustained but their relationship is constantly under strain, because of their fear that Mrs Burman will expose the irregularity of their union and so harm their daughter, Nesta (as well as undermining Victor's social supremacy). By the end of the book Mrs Burman is dead, Natalie is dead, Victor is mad, and Nesta has survived a broken engagement and gone forward into a happy marriage. The tragic essence of the work lies in the deeply intimate married relationship which is both intensified and diminished by fear. Meredith attempts to combine this theme with mordant comedy concerning society, the cash-nexus, flaccid imperialism, and attitudes to class and religion. The meeting point of social and private concerns is in Victor's unreflective sensibility.

The book opens with a scene which combines stream-of-consciousness and comic incident to curious effect. Victor Radnor, crossing London Bridge,

> was almost magically detached from his conflict with the gale by some sly strip of slipperiness, abounding in that conduit of the markets, which had more or less adroitly performed the trick on preceding passengers, and now laid this one flat amid the shuffle of feet, peaceful for the moment as the uncomplaining who have gone to Sabrina beneath the tides.

The animistic dream-like imagery and the elliptical suggestion of events provide a way in to Victor's consciousness, while retaining the objective, organised form of the narrator's voice. The scene as a whole prefigures the catastrophe that finally overtakes him. He is helped up after his fall by a working man who dirties his waistcoat. Victor, condescendingly laughing off his annoyance, is rebuked by another workman: 'and none of your dam punctilio'.[4] The phrase echoes through the book; Victor's gesture of touching with two fingers the back of his head where he fell becomes a premonition of madness. Both phrase and gesture are associated with the great 'Idea' which came to him in his fall and which he forever struggles to regain and never reaches, though fragmentary glimpses of it come at intervals.

The episode is central to the meaning of the novel: Meredith takes one of the crudest and most irresistible of jokes and uses it directly against the grain of our primitive response to it. A dignified gentleman slips on a fruit peel. Beneath the tour-de-force of presenting the scene through Victor's consciousness (which sees the episode as perturbing, irritating, even menacing, never as comic) there remains the residue of simple incident with its stock response. This sets limits to our identification with Victor—who sees himself as without limits. An appraising distance is placed between reader and character by the undertow of comedy, while our direct entry into his stream of consciousness absorbs us into the hero's tragedy.

All Meredith's novels expressly exploit the relativity of comedy and tragedy. He sees them—as in the scene just analysed—not as dealing with different *orders* of experience but as representing different *attitudes* towards it. He connects these attitudes to the different levels of personality in his characters: his recurrent image of the 'two men' within us does not set man's spiritual against his animal nature. It expresses the conflict between a man's rationalised image of himself and his self in action:

'So well do we know ourselves, that we one and all determine to know a purer', says the heroine of my columns. Philosophy in fiction tells, among various other matters, of the perils of this intimate acquaintance with a flattering familiar in the 'purer'—a person who more than ceases to be of use to us after his ideal shall have led up men from their flint and arrowhead caverns to inter-communicative daylight. For when the fictitious creature has performed that service of helping to civilize the world, it becomes the most dangerous of delusions, causing first the individual to despise the mass, and then to join the mass in crushing the individual. (*Diana of the Crossways*, i; 19)

Meredith shows that the failure to recognise the disparity between these two selves is the source of that confusion which can, equally, produce comic and tragic results. He identifies the comic attitude with reason's control and hence with retrospection; the tragic attitude with involvement and action and hence with the continuous present. The two attitudes are shown jarring against each other and it is their friction, rather than any reconciliation between them, which generates the energy of his novels.

Meredith presents the habitually irreconcilable views of experience: that of those who have undergone it and know its confusion and agony and patternlessness, and that of those who look on, to whom the experience seems limpidly and satisfyingly diagrammatic. One of the most peculiar features of his approach is his way of presenting an incident concurrently as fully comic and fully tragic. Willoughby's jealous torment in *The Egoist* is presented in language whose intensity is not destroyed by the sharp wit of the narrator's comments. Victor Radnor's disintegration is dogged by his fruitless attempt to recapture the 'Idea' (which momentarily illuminated him when he slipped on a banana skin). The effect is not one of irony, for this implies equilibrium. Meredith veers disquietingly between two poles, avoiding either tragedy's commitment to experience or the 'point fixe' of comedy. The reader is forced to undertake simultaneously two contradictory roles: that of living through the experience and that of analysing it dispassionately.

Throughout his creative life Meredith recognised (at times unwillingly) how narrow is the sphere of reason within human personality. Constantly in his later novels his characters are confronted with the limits of their reason and control. Comedy, which in his work yokes together analysis and action, is Meredith's method of instruction: 'the brainstuff of fiction is internal history' (*Diana*, i; 17), but the 'inner I' may delude, to understand fully we must examine 'the material points of her conduct—indicators of the spiritual secret always. What are the patient's acts?' (*Diana*, xviii; 206). The method is, strictly, anti-realistic. Within the novels he shows how difficult it is for men to recognise the nature of their actions; he forces on the reader-as-character (though not always on the character) the act of recognition.

In the late eighteen-seventies Meredith explored the idea of comedy in a variety of works—short stories ('The House on the Beach' and 'The Case of General Ople and Lady Camper'), an unpublished drama, 'The Satirist', the *Essay* and two novels, *The Egoist* and *The Tragic Comedians*. Through these works he elucidated his own vision of comedy and defined its limits. In *The Tragic Comedians* he wrote a work which annihilated comedy. 'Comedians' is the detached general description of the characters, 'Tragic' the adjectival particular. Never again after 1880 did he write a novel in which the comic was the controlling ethos.

On 1 February 1877 Meredith delivered a lecture which later became known as *An Essay on Comedy and the Uses of the Comic Spirit*. The essay was printed in the *New Quarterly Magazine* in April 1877, but first separately published in 1897, when it was reviewed by Bernard Shaw.[5] Although its general critical influence was delayed, its composition was artistically crucial for Meredith himself. Meredith's own avowed favourite among his novels, *Beauchamp's Career*, was written during the preceding years, and *The Egoist*, which immediately succeeds the *Essay*, is often taken to be his masterpiece.

Many of the effects in *The Egoist* can be traced directly to Meredith's theories on comedy, and its introductory chapter presents an epitome of the main ideas of the *Essay*. Meredith creates a rather laboured comic detachment by presenting the ideas in a burlesque of Carlyle's style and then explaining them to us in his own somewhat similar and equally idiosyncratic manner. In the *Essay* Meredith elaborated at length, and with examples drawn from many strands of European literature, the idea that true comedy was 'the fountain of sound sense' and that the comic spirit was directed against 'Unreason and Sentimentalism'. In *The Egoist* he warned those who would be free from the scrutiny of the comic spirit: 'Do not offend reason' (Prelude, p. 4). The imps of comedy malignly 'love to uncover ridiculousness in imposing figures' (Prelude, p. 5). Comedy is concerned to correct pretensions and exaggerations, not to laugh at genuine emotion, though 'A lover pretending too much by one foot's length of pretence, will have that foot caught in her trap' (Prelude, p. 4). Comedy must be distinguished from humour and from satire: it is more intellectual than humour, less derisive than satire. 'Incidents of a kind casting ridicule on our unfortunate nature instead of our conventional life, provoke derisive laughter, which thwarts the Comic idea. But derision is foiled by the play of the intellect' (*Essay*). It is 'the play of the intellect' which Meredith uses as his primary weapon of comedy in *The Egoist*.

Two minor works which he wrote while thinking out the *Essay* shed light on its implications for him as an artist. Meredith had already begun to test his critical formulations through the stresses of writing an original work. The unpublished play 'The Satirist', is particularly relevant because it was written during the time that Meredith was at work on the *Essay*.[6] One of the *Essay*'s themes is Meredith's attempt to differentiate comedy from both humour and satire:

The Comic, which is the perceptive, is the governing spirit, awakening and giving aim to these powers of laughter, but it is not to be confounded with them: it enfolds a thinner form of them, differing from satire, in not sharply driving into the quivering sensibilities, and from humour, in not comforting them and tucking them up, or indicating a broader than the range of this bustling world to them. (*Essay*)

Whereas comedy appeals to reason and exhibits folly only in order to cure it, satire appeals to more murderous instincts: 'The laughter of satire is a blow in the back or the face.' Instead of the 'sunny malice' of the comic spirit, satire 'smells of carrion'. Meredith describes Alceste in Molière's *Le Misanthrope* in this way:

He is that melancholy person, the critic of everybody save himself; intensely sensitive to the faults of others, wounded by them; in love with his own indubitable honesty, and with his ideal of the simpler form of life befitting it: qualities which constitute the satirist. (*Essay*)

Raphael, the hero of 'The Satirist', strikingly resembles this character sketch. The play explores in dramatic human terms the central discussion of the *Essay*: What is the function of the comic poet in society? The play is incomplete but coherent: it consists of a hundred consecutive holograph pages forming fourteen scenes of Act I of the drama: its theme seems fully worked out. Perhaps Meredith abandoned it because he had expressed the idea of the work in the extremely long first act. The play's theme is the way in which the hero discovers his responsibility for the consequences of his destructive attitude towards society. Raphael, the Satirist, thinks himself superior to the corrupt society in which he lives: in the course of the play he is forced to see that he is himself a part of its corruption. Raphael is accused of killing a young nobleman, Octavius, in a duel—the evidence is that the assailant had taunted Octavius with satirical verses written by Raphael. Raphael denies all responsibility and refuses to flee: he is confronted by Amatista, Octavius's betrothed, with whom he has himself had an equivocal relationship (she in fact, during a period of estrangement, had persuaded him to write the verses against Octavius). At last, he discovers that the killer of Octavius was Manuel, his own disciple, and that Octavius believed that he was fighting Raphael. Abandoned by his employer, Don Beltran, Raphael cryptically obeys a summons to appear before the king. The manuscript ends with this exchange:

Raphael: Ten minutes with the King!
Manuel: You're lost.
Raphael: Made! Made!
There do I quit the ladder and plant foot
Upon the highest stage, and there begins
(End of manuscript)

We are left uncertain what 'begins'—is it material advantage, or the status of tragic hero? The second would be a more emotionally satisfying solution, but the unfulfilled dénouement makes it impossible fully to judge the play's meaning. Meredith's attitude to his villain-hero remains ambiguous. Perhaps it was this basic ambiguity of feeling which made it impossible for him to finish the play as a '5 Act comedy in verse': the comic spirit which could see Raphael's predicament as material for comedy would be savage indeed, and yet, in terms of Meredith's philosophy, Raphael's Timonesque bitterness cannot be shown as a heroic force. As it stands, the play shows how irresponsible any attempt to condemn the world must be if we remain disengaged from society. The theme is taken up in a different way in Willoughby's desire to banish the world.

Meredith is again exploring, in dramatic form, two of his most insistent themes: the need for a harmonious balance between instinct and reason; and, second, the ease with which we see through others while remaining blind about ourselves. The function of comedy, as he sees it, is to show us the true nature of our actions—particularly those acts of impulse and self-seeking which appear to us disguised as reason and 'good citizenship'. The issue of 'good citizenship' is fraught with artistic difficulties, and Meredith did not solve them all. The fruitful relationship of the comic poet to society is everywhere asserted in the *Essay*. He says there that it is necessary to believe that

> our state of society is founded in common-sense, otherwise you will not be struck by the contrasts the Comic Spirit perceives, or have it to look to for your consolation. You will, in fact, be standing in that peculiar oblique beam of light, yourself illuminated to the general eye as the very object of chase and doomed quarry of the thing obscure to you. But to feel its presence and to see it is your assurance that many sane and solid minds are with you in what you are experiencing: and this of itself spares you the pain of satirical heat, and the bitter craving to strike heavy blows.

By setting 'The Satirist' in Spain, Meredith immediately complicated the issue: Raphael is plainly living in a society *not* founded on common sense and so is unable to find any 'sweet pleasant juice of contrast'. He feels himself isolated and develops 'the bitter craving to strike heavy blows'. He becomes a destructive anti-rational force and the result is lurid melodrama instead of the 'clear reason' of comedy. Apart from the first scene (which is in prose), the play is almost entirely un-comic. It shows the tragic result of misusing the weapons of comedy.

A major criticism which has been made of Meredith's theory of comedy is that he placed too much faith in the *status quo*; society is seen as the norm and any sharp deviation opens the culprit to chastisement by the comic spirit. This attitude is not always carried through in the novels, but it is certainly part of his thought in the *Essay*. The construction of 'The Satirist' places it closer to the *Essay* than to a novel like *The Tragic Comedians* where the hero is ruined by attempting to come to terms with bourgeois society. In 'The Satirist' Meredith sets the play in an environment where there are implied grounds for the wrath of the satirist, but he does not follow up this hint. He says in the *Essay*: 'The

Satirist is moral agent, often a social scavenger, working on a storage of bile'—but Raphael is denied any adequate focus for his anger until he experiences injustice personally. Moreover, he is himself involved in the corruption of the time (for example, in his relations with Amatista). We never know what Raphael wrote in his satires or what are the particular abuses of the people against whom Raphael directs his spleen. The implication is that Raphael is actuated by petty motives—but this is never proved. By thus undermining the moral position of his satirist hero, Meredith avoids the question of the satirist's duty in a corrupt society.

While preparing the *Essay on Comedy* Meredith studied the works of Aristophanes and several pages of his working manuscript notes, apparently written about that time, are preserved in the Altschul collection.[7] In Aristophanes he was confronted with 'a lusty and strong-smelling wit', but he says of him: 'He was not only a satirist: he was a critic of politicians, poets, philosophers.' The rather curious antithesis in this sentence is to some extent explained by his marginal comparison with 'Our English Foote' who 'was a meaner kind of Aristophanes, and with some garlic in him, but none of the sacred fire, and no sense of public interests'. The sacred fire and the sense of public interests are also lacking in Raphael. I think it more likely that Meredith's hostility to satire in the *Essay* derives to some extent from his feelings towards his own creation, Raphael, than that Raphael is purely a dramatic projection of Meredith's views on satire. With a writer like Meredith, whose characters existed to him as living beings, the passage of ideas is two-way; the comedy may 'be in the idea' but the characters who figure forth the idea become human beings to whom the author then reacts emotionally—as he reacts to Sir Willoughby. Raphael is satisfactory only as an individual representing one kind of satirical impulse. He is not an adequate criticism of the function of satire itself.

As so often in Meredith's work, one feels the urgency of

a personal argument in the way he explores the implications of satire both in the *Essay* and the play. His own position had some affinities with that of Raphael: like him he had felt the pain of isolation which brings with it the 'craving to strike heavy blows'; he had himself been accused of cynicism, and there is a considerable element of cruelty in his comedies, particularly those of the late eighteen-seventies such as 'General Ople and Lady Camper' and *The Egoist*. Yet he admired Molière's wit most because 'it is full of healing'. In a letter later in his life to an American admirer (15 November 1886) he defended himself against the charge of cynicism: 'There has been a confounding of the tone of irony (or satire in despair) with cynicism. I must have overcharged the dose to produce such an impression' (*Letters*, ii, 387). 'Satire in despair' well describes Raphael's speech of self-discovery. In Raphael Meredith embodied his own temptations towards the contempt of society which he rebukes in the *Essay* and for which he reproves himself some ten years later in a letter to George Stevenson (15 January 1888): 'Without placing myself high—or anywhere—I am, I moan to think, disdainful of an English public, and am beset with devils of satire when I look on it. That is not a good state for composition' (*Letters*, ii, 406). This determination to reject Raphael's intellectual position while feeling an unwilling emotional sympathy with him enriches the ambiguity of characterisation in the play; but it may also account for its unfinished state.

The short story 'The Case of General Ople and Lady Camper' is the most doctrinaire 'comedy' among his works, and it is correspondingly less successful as fiction. The story describes the persecution of General Ople by his eccentric neighbour, Lady Camper. General Ople is a retired officer well pleased with life, 'in good humour with himself', and given to genteel phrases. Blinded by his own wishes, he believes that Lady Camper, socially his superior, is favourably inclined to receiving a marriage proposal from him. In fact she is concerned only to prevent the intimacy between his daughter and her nephew which General Ople has failed to notice. Lady Camper goes abroad and sends a fleet of cartoons to the General, each showing him in a ridiculous situation and emphasising his self-importance. The twist which makes the story more than a malicious retailing of a practical joke is that General Ople is obscurely flattered as well as hurt by her attentions and cannot resist showing the cartoons around the neighbourhood, rousing ridicule and pity among his acquaintances. Lady Camper's function is corrective. When she has finally reduced his self-esteem and persuaded him to think of his daughter Elizabeth before himself, she marries him. Such is her acuteness that: 'The senses of General Ople were struck by the aspect of a lurid Goddess, who penetrated him, read him through, and had both power and will to expose and make him ridiculous for ever' (vi; 163). Lady Camper clearly has the functions of the Comic Spirit, and she claims that she exaggerates only in order to bring home the truth: 'Could any caricature of mine exceed in grotesque your sketch of yourself? You are a brave and generous man all the same: and I suspect it is more hoodwinking than egotism—or extreme egotism—that blinds you' (viii; 183). This speech gives us the clue to what is wrong with the story. Throughout we see things from the general's point of view. Lady Camper remains remote, her motives obscure, whereas we are made to feel that he is indeed a 'brave and generous man' driven to the verge of insanity by an apparently pointless persecution. The punishment he undergoes is ludicrously out of proportion to the crime, and though this may be true to tragedy, to life, and to the comedy of buffoonery, it runs counter to the 'comic spirit' because it arouses an atmosphere of hysteria, not of reasonableness. It is true that in the *Essay* Meredith wrote that 'keen-edged intelligence is by nature merciless' and that some of the highest comedy 'refines even to pain'. Nevertheless by giving one of his characters the impregnable position and power of the comic spirit, he alienates our sympathies from her. There is too much unacknowledged and unsatirised self-esteem in Lady Camper for us to enjoy her triumph.

In this story Meredith faces the problem, even more acute in *The Egoist*, inherent in his metaphor for the Idea of comedy.

> For Folly is the natural prey of the Comic, known to it in all her transformations, in every disguise; and it is with the springing delight of hawk over heron, hound after fox, that it gives her chase, never fretting, never tiring, sure of having her, allowing her no rest.

The reader is predisposed to feel sympathy for the hunted rather than the hunter, and although this can serve a satiric purpose by making the reader undergo the character's punishment, he must be convinced that the punishment is just.

These two works test certain of the *Essay*'s assertions in action, but they are limited in scope and achievement—curiously less humane than the *Essay* itself. Though this is presented as an attempt to *define* comedy, the method used is poetic: it works through metaphor and paradox, illuminating the comic spirit by its closeness to it, rather than by building a close-structured argument. It is a *representation* of the spirit of comedy.

Meredith's description of the comic spirit sheds light on his attitude as narrator in *The Egoist*, his 'comedy in narrative' as he sub-titled it. *The Egoist* was his first full-length novel after writing the *Essay*. He had begun it by June 1877, and finished it by the middle of February 1879, at a heavy cost to his health. 'The Satirist' was written from about August 1876 to some time after April 1877. 'The House on the Beach' which he had begun fifteen years ealier was recast and appeared in the *New Quarterly* in January 1877. 'The Case of General Ople and Lady Camper', printed in the *New Quarterly*, July 1877, was probably written during the April in which the *Essay* was published. During the two months after finishing *The Egoist* Meredith wrote a draft of the first quarter of *The Amazing Marriage* which he was not to finish until 1894. All these works represent in some degree his changing attitude to comedy.

In *The Egoist* he examines many of the epitomised observations of the *Essay* against the shifting world of human personalities and relationships. The book is his only attempt to write a sustained 'comedy' invoking the conventions of the stage, and particularly of Molière's comedies, the source of whose wit, Meredith says, is pure reason. 'He strips Folly to the skin, displays the imposture of the creature, and is content to offer her better clothing'; that is, as he says in *The Egoist*, 'In Comedy is the singular scene of charity issuing of disdain under the stroke of honourable laughter'.

The comedy he most often cites in the *Essay* is *Le Misanthrope*, and this has some obvious plot connections with *The Egoist*: it is about an unfulfilled engagement, and one in which the hero, although a good man, makes demands upon the heroine which it is impossible for her to fulfil without running counter to her nature. Just as the first cause of the dissension between Sir Willoughby and Clara is his wish to banish the world, so that between Alceste and Célimène is his wish to retire into a deserted countryside far from the corruptions of the court. Just as Sir Willoughby offers his hand to Laetitia, so Alceste attempts at one point to revenge himself on Célimène by proposing marriage to her cousin, who is devoted to him. Here however the resemblance ends. Alceste is shown as truly (and unreasonably) in love with Célimène, whereas we see nothing of the relationship of the lovers in *The Egoist* until Clara's withdrawal has begun. The suggestion is that there has never been any relationship. The attitude of the two writers to their characters has less in common than might at first appear: Molière is the more truly reasonable because more truly charitable. Alceste is endearing as well as infuriating, whereas there is a coldness in Sir Willoughby and in Meredith's treatment of him which creates an effect of cruelty. Meredith gives himself the position of comic spirit—detached, disengaged; but he uses it in a way that sometimes seems self-flagellatory and reminds us that Sir Willoughby represents much that Meredith wants to drive out of himself as well as others.

The effect of near-hysteria in parts of *The Egoist* does not, of course, derive always from autobiographical pressures; it is also a dramatisation of Clara's state of mind. Meredith's apparent detachment from the characters in *The Egoist* (he is even at a distance from the comic imps) helps him to keep the control which he admired in Molière, but the violent image he uses to describe Molière's achievement suggests the enormous self-discipline needed to retain his impartiality: 'Never did man wield so shrieking a scourge upon vice, but his consummate self-mastery is not shaken while administering it'. Molière's comedies support Meredith in his attempt to reach ideal comic detachment: 'the laughter of reason refreshed' (*Egoist*, Prelude).

Robert Louis Stevenson reports that when a young friend complained that Meredith had based Sir Willoughby on him, Meredith replied, 'No, my dear fellow, he is all of us'.[8] But Meredith's other comments on the book suggest that he felt that Sir Willoughby did not represent the whole of us. He wrote to Stevenson on 16 April 1879: 'It is a comedy with only half of me in it' (*Letters*, i, 297), and to Foote he wrote: 'It comes mainly from the head and has nothing to kindle imagination' (*Letters*, i, 300). Allowing for Meredith's usual dissatisfaction with recently finished work, these comments show how oppressed he was by the narrow intensity of the book's form. Its power derives from a sense of barely, exquisitely, contained emotion.

The Egoist becomes an exploration of the boundaries beyond which comedy cannot venture. 'Life, we know too well, is not a Comedy, but something strangely mixed', he wrote in the *Essay*; *The Egoist* ranges beyond what Meredith had earlier declared to be the province of comedy: social follies rather than man's inescapable nature. 'Do not offend reason', enjoin *Essay* and Prelude—but as soon as Meredith is dealing with human figures he shows a heightened consciousness of how narrow is reason's power in human conduct: and he sees further that since the flouting of reason is the root of comedy, comedy may have a tragic issue in the lives of human beings. When the control of reason is removed, the result may be the ludicrous spectacle of Tinman in 'The House on the Beach' adorning himself in his court suit for his private admiration, or it may equally be the hideous frenzy of Alvan in *The Tragic Comedians* struggling against ever-increasing odds to regain his loved Clotilde. The entirely reasonable man is quite as likely to be a cold self-seeker, like Cecil Baskelett in *Beauchamp's Career* who can only see *through* men, as he is to be a self-abnegating rational lover, like Vernon Whitford in *The Egoist*. Although tragedy is not in question, the special emotional edge of *The Egoist* comes from a sense of poignancy held at bay.

The narrative language represents the characters' active inner life and sets it off against their elaborately controlled dialogue exchanges.

An example to which *The Westminster Review* took exception in its notice of *The Egoist* is the passage in which Laetitia Dale has her first unwilling doubts about Sir Willoughby's perfection. Having engaged her affections without declaring his, he has abruptly left for a three year trip abroad. On his return he greets her enthusiastically but withdraws again and some time later Laetitia is told by young Crossjaye that he has seen Willoughby riding with a young lady fifteen miles away.

Still . . . the tale seemed fictitious to Laetitia until Crossjay related how that he had stood to salute on the road to the railway, and taken off his cap to Sir Willoughby, and Sir Willoughby had passed him, not noticing him, though the young lady did, and looked back and nodded. The hue of truth was in that picture.

Strange eclipse, when the hue of truth comes shadowing over our bright ideal planet. It will not seem the planet's fault, but truth's. Reality is the offender; delusion our treasure that we are robbed of. Then begins with us the term of wilful delusion, and its necessary accompaniment of the disgust of reality; exhausting the heart much more than patient endurance of starvation. (iv; 35)

The Westminster Review says that the last paragraph quoted is 'wrapping up such a simple, we might almost say common-place, proposition in such mysterious terms' and dismisses Meredith as 'over-fastidious, or what the world would vulgarly call too clever'.[9] The general truth conveyed *may* be common-place (that we prefer to be deluded rather than face unpleasant truth): but through the image of the eclipse 'shadowing over our bright ideal planet' Meredith also renders the intensity of this ordinary truth when it is actually experienced.[10] The darkening of the sky, the chilling greyness of familiar objects, the forebodings associated with eclipse: these are suggested in order to convey Laetitia's feelings at that moment. Sir Willoughby is her planet, and the silent overcasting is also the emotional process within Laetitia which goes unrecognised in speech and finds an issue into consciousness only much later in the novel. The half-submerged violence of the image of appetite and starvation is the end of a sequence suggesting the voracious emotion which Laetitia always suppresses in her active life. When Sir Willoughby seems to be returning to her,

The starveling of patience awoke to the idea of a feast. The sense of hunger came with it, and hope came, and patience fled.

He leaves her again:

Patience travelled back to her sullenly. As we must have some kind of food, and she had nothing else, she took to that and found it dryer than of yore. It is a composing but a lean dietary. The dead are patient, and we get a certain likeness to them in feeding on it unintermittingly overlong. (iv; 31)

The grandiloquence of the comparison with the dead allows Laetitia's despair its full stature. Through metaphor we are made inward with her. Instead of hearing a well worn story about a stock figure—the blue-stocking, slightly faded, devoted spinster—we enter into the quality of her experience. This has other effects in the book: we are made to see the crassness of Sir Willoughby's conventional view of her and are further alienated from him. By devoting a chapter to Laetitia's inner life so early in the book, Meredith awakens our sympathetic understanding of her so that he is able to assume her life for much of the rest of the time. The structural tour-de-force praised by E. M. Forster in *Aspects of the Novel* draws heavily on this early vein of imagery.[11] When Laetitia at last declares her changed feelings for Willoughby we can greet the stroke not with incredulity but with delighted recognition.

Meredith says in the *Essay* that comedy does not deal with 'periods of fervour' but in the novel both Clara and Willoughby are in a state of ferment, swelling beneath the glossy surface of polite interchange in which a raised eyebrow is the only possible representation of rage. The basis of the novel is the struggle between the instinctual demands of a man or woman's nature and the social forms they adopt by demand or as disguise. The struggle is not judged easily: Meredith believes in civilisation and evolution. What he shows is that a man like Willoughby may use the forms of civilisation to disguise from himself an uncontained and animal voraciousness, and that the same civilised forms may prevent a woman like Clara from responding in her own full identity because they present her with a model of what a lady should feel and be—a model which is static and anti-evolutionary.

The clash takes its crucial form in the disparity between the pre-ordained conventional patterns of fiction and actual existential feeling. Sir Willoughby Patterne is a 'model' gentleman ('He has a leg', as Mrs Mountstuart cryptically observes). He is the ideal hero of popular Victorian fiction—handsome, intelligent, wealthy, generous, and admired by all about him. Clara, the girl to whom he is engaged, seems to have all the qualities of a typical novel heroine: she is pretty, absolutely 'pure' and inexperienced sexually, with means of her own and the only daughter of an elderly scholar-gentleman. Everyone is preparing for a conventional courtship and wedding. But this is an anti-conventional novel which takes the easy expectations of society and the plot judgments of fiction and turns them askew. Thus, Clara who has been swept off her feet by Willoughby's romantic whirlwind courtship begins to realise that whirlwind courtships may be a form of aggression and a prelude to annihilation. She comes to understand (all unwillingly) that Sir Willoughby's ideal of marriage is not partnership but absorption. The narrator interprets Willoughby's view of it thus:

She would not burn the world for him; she would not, though a purer poetry is little imaginable, reduce herself to ashes, or incense, or essence, in honour of him, and so, by love's transmutation, literally be the man she was to marry. She preferred to be herself, with the egoism of women! She said it: she said: 'I must be myself to be of any value to you, Willoughby.' (vi; 54)

He uses everyone to act as a flattering mirror for himself and is incapable of dialogue:

'So entirely one, that there never can be question of external influences. I am, we will say, riding home from the hunt: I see you awaiting me: I read your heart as though you were beside me. And I know that I am coming to the one who reads mine! You have me, you have me like an open book, you, and only you!'

'I am to be always at home?' Clara said, unheeded, and relieved by his not hearing. (vii; 73)

Meeting his faithful first love, Laetitia, after a journey abroad of three years, this is how he greets her:

'Laetitia Dale!' he said. He panted. 'Your name is sweet English

> music! And you are well?' The anxious question permitted him to read deeply in her eyes. He found the man he sought there, squeezed him passionately, and let her go . . .' (iv; 29–30)

Clara's growing dislike of Willoughby's possessiveness develops into a sullen physical antagonism. She cannot bear him to kiss her.

> The gulf of a caress hove in view like an enormous billow hollowing under the curled ridge.
>
> She stooped to a buttercup; the monster swept by. (xiii; 153)

These passages show the range of strategies by which the reader is led to judge Sir Willoughby; the representation of his consciousness in which his thoughts and the narrator's overlap; direct speech; motives imputed to him by an epitomising commentator; mock-heroic aggrandising metaphor. Willoughby is indeed pursued.

Meredith does not entirely avoid rousing our sympathy for Sir Willoughby by the end of the book. As he says in the Prelude: 'The Egoist surely inspires pity. He who would desire to clothe himself at everybody's expense, and is of that desire condemned to strip himself stark naked, he, if pathos ever had a form, might be taken for the actual person.' What makes us stand apart from Sir Willoughby, even while feeling the ironic truth of this passage, is that the last thing he himself wants is to rouse pity. Most of his activity in the second half of the book is part of the effort to save face, to allow the world no opportunity to pity him. Meredith denies him tragic stature by allowing him to be successful in his efforts. The book ends with him handing Clara over to the cousin whom he still sees as inferior to himself, discomfiting his friend De Craye who has tried to get Clara, and presenting Laetitia to a not entirely sceptical world as his inescapable destiny. He remains much the same man at the end as he was at the beginning. The Comedy has corrected but not reclaimed him. Although the function of comedy is 'to teach the world what ails it', it never really teaches Sir Willoughby.

If the reader's role is to be primarily that of judge, it is necessary that our detachment should be sustained. Meredith's usual method of rousing and flouting our expectations has to be modified. Elsewhere he emphasises the devious flow of life, the often undynamic nature of significant emotion, the pressure of free will on circumstances and of circumstances on individuality, and in his later works he begins to abandon belief in congruity of character. In some of his novels where he claims to be writing internal history, such as *Sandra Belloni*, recognisable plot patterns are more or less obliterated, while in others he uses patterns the reader will recognise but which give only a deliberately limited insight into the conduct of the action. Only in *The Egoist* does he use reassuring analogues within the work whose promise is fulfilled: our concern for Clara is tempered because we have been told at the outset that the book is 'a comedy in narrative': because Sir Willoughby's previous, ironically-named fiancée, Constantia, escaped, and because we know that he is selfish before Clara does.

The book begins with the episode of the valiant but unromantically plebeian and middle-aged sailor Patterne to whom Willoughby is 'not at home'—because he does not fit the dashing version of him that Willoughby has been purveying to the county. This man is the father of young Crossjaye who acts in the novel as the touchstone of character other than the test of love. Love is not the only, though the most fiery, test men meet: social relationships test too. By using a prepubertal child to test the behaviour of his characters, Meredith can subject them to different demands.

Besides the analogues within the novel, Meredith suggests several other parallels to give the reader a sense of control and detachment and to avoid an avid emotional involvement in the characters' experience. The areas of disturbance are clearly defined: the shocks the reader undergoes, such as Laetitia's change of mind, are in part foreseen. There is the satisfying congruity of promise and performance, a stability larger than the individual surprises, which is common to classical comic novels. Fielding's comic masterpieces *Joseph Andrews* and *Tom Jones* have this kind of dependable harmony.

One foresight into the plot is on the whole lost to modern readers: the clue given us in Sir Willoughby Patterne's name. R. D. Mayo pointed out in his article '*The Egoist* and the Willow Pattern' that not only is there the element of Pattern (a model of manhood); there is also a reference to the Willow Pattern story.[12] This story, constructed from the figures on the popular blue willow pattern plate, runs thus: a widower mandarin intends to marry his daughter to a wealthy suitor but the maiden chooses a poor but honourable man serving as her father's secretary. She and the secretary escape, hotly pursued by father and betrothed and are turned into birds for their fidelity. The story had been used as the basis of a successful pantomime in 1875 by Francis Burnand, editor of *Punch* and a close friend of Meredith. In the novel Clara's father, the mandarin-scholar, Dr Middleton, is determined that she shall marry Willoughby, while during the course of the book we see her gradually awakening feeling for Vernon Whitford, Willoughby's scholar-secretary.

The parallels are clear though not insistent. The willow-pattern analogue gives a meaningful edge to the persistent references to porcelain throughout the story. Mrs Mountstuart perturbs Willoughby by harping on her definition of Clara as 'a dainty rogue in porcelain' and (gnomic as ever) refusing to explain herself. Austin Dobson's 'Proverbs in Porcelain', French-style amorous dialogues, appeared in 1877, two years before *The Egoist*, and these, I think, may be another pointer to Willoughby's unease. Colonel de Craye, Sir Willoughby's friend who hopes to win Clara from him, brings a wedding present of a porcelain vase which is immediately smashed in an accident on the way from the station—and here Meredith may be invoking echoes from

Restoration and Augustan comedy: the famous double-entendre scene of 'viewing the china' in Wycherley's *The Country Wife*, Pope's image in *The Rape of the Lock*:

> Whether the nymph shall break Diana's law,
> Or some frail china-jar receive a flaw.

Towards the end of the book Clara's unwillingness to accept a china dinner-service reveals to the county gossips her unwillingness to go through with the marriage. The willow-pattern story and the images from porcelain work together with exacerbating significance: they are an additional emotional restraint on us as readers because they give us controlling knowledge, but the nagging repetition of the porcelain imagery grates after a time in a way which makes us share something of Sir Willoughby's exasperation.

For although our sympathy is in the main invited for Clara, Meredith is too subtle an observer to refuse a measure of fellow-feeling to Willoughby or to suggest that he has a monopoly of egoism. 'The love-season is the carnival of egoism, and brings the touchstone to our natures' (xi; 130). Meredith is showing the workings of egoism in *all* his characters and particularly in Clara, and in this way he suggests that egoism is common to us all. Nor does he suggest that egotism is *necessarily* destructive. In the youthful Crossjaye, egotism is part of a sturdy, growing identity and the other characters are judged by their response to his demands. Vernon wants to send him to train in London at his own expense because it is best for the boy; Laetitia behaves like an anxious, upright mother towards him; Willoughby spoils him but is ready to abandon him if he goes against his wishes (as he has done the wretched Flitch and will do Vernon if he leaves); Clara delights him and uses him in her escape. She forgets him (having bound him to wait for her by a childish obsessional promise) and she plays on his awakening sexuality.

Laetitia's declaration at the end of the book, 'I am an

Egoist', is a declaration of growth as well as of hardening. Her timid self-abnegation has given way to independence. Clara's egotism is inextricable from her discovery of her self, which includes her sexual self—and *The Egoist* is exceptional among Victorian novels in the closeness and intensity with which it suggests sexual revulsion (just as *The Tragic Comedians* is exceptional in the ferocity with which it depicts sexual obsession). Clara realises 'the tragedy of the embrace' which will come to her if she dutifully fulfils her engagement and 'the clash of a sharp physical thought: "The difference! the difference!" told her she was woman and never could submit' (xxi; 239). In this struggle 'physical pride' and 'incandescent reason' unite to affirm her distinctness—while at the same time they lead her to understand how essential love is to her.

> With her body straining in her dragon's grasp, with the savour of loathing, unable to contend, unable to speak aloud, she began to speak to herself, and all the health of her nature made her outcry womanly:—'If I were loved!'—not for the sake of love, but for free breathing; and her utterance of it was to ensure life and enduringness to the wish, as the yearning of a mother on a drowning ship is to get her infant to shore. (x; 120)

To Willoughby the essentially feminine is 'a parasite—a chalice': Clara's twistings, false starts, half lies have, in contrast, the hectic serpentine movement of the hunted. She is saved from Willoughby's portentous self-absorption not only by her capacity to love but by her humour. Meredith's language to describe her is similar to his description of the comic spirit: 'her equable shut mouth threw its long curve to guard the small round chin from that effect; her eyes wavered only in humour' (v; 46). But her close resemblance to the spirit of the work ('that slim feasting smile, shaped like the long-bow') does not protect her from the consequences of her human complexity.

The book is an intricate account of the duel between Willoughby and Clara: neither of them is a particularly scrupulous fighter. Both are fighting defensively to preserve the same thing: their identity. Willoughby *cannot* release Clara from her engagement because his love for her is intimately entangled with his assurance of his own worth—if she goes he will no longer be Sir Willoughby Patterne, cynosure of the county, but a twice-jilted man. Clara *cannot* marry Willoughby to be absorbed by his voracious love. Although the original cause of his dispute with Clara is his vaunted wish to 'banish the world' and live in total absorbed intimacy with her, he is really entirely dependent on the world's estimate of him. He exists to himself only through the mirror image it reflects of him, and his relationship with Clara was to have been a rosy and enlarging mirror—extending his image beyond death.

Clara 'was the first who taught him what it was to have sensations of his mortality' (xxiii; 279). The concerns of the book are lofty and the suffering of the characters is allowed its full stature and inwardness. We *realise* the experience of Willoughby's self-pity through the imagery:

> This was the ground of his hatred of the world: it was an appalling fear on behalf of his naked eidolon, the tender infant Self swaddled in his name before the world, for which he felt as the most highly civilised of men alone can feel, and which it was impossible for him to stretch out hands to protect. There the poor little loveable creature ran for any mouth to blow on; and frost-nipped and bruised, it cried to him, and he was of no avail! (xxix; 344)

(This is strikingly close to the imagery used by Clara, in the passage quoted above.) The mingling of parental tenderness and infantilism measures both the intensity and the inadequacy of Willoughby's capacity to love. The ultimate thinness and repetitiveness of his characterisation is seen to represent the actual thinness and repetitiveness of egotism.[13]

The book is long (about 600 pages): it may seem an excessive length for the breaking of an engagement—even so solemn a betrothal as Willoughby has enforced. Until two-thirds of the way through there is little physical action. This is partly because Willoughby owns everything within sight except the railway; Clara's flight to the railway station is in itself an assertion of freedom. Her vision of the Alps is the only glimpse of a free world beyond the confines of the book. In contrast to the lush, privately-owned landscape of the home-counties is set the crystalline freedom of the mountains. The length of the book corresponds to the density of the emotional life described: it is swift, not leisurely, but 'The slave of a passion thinks in a ring, as hares run: he will cease where he began' (xxiii; 272). The claustrophobia of the relationship between Willoughby and Clara, which is the cause of its dissolution, also makes it almost impossible to dissolve.

In order to underline the claustrophobic effect Meredith follows a form of three unities: the action is continuous, in one place, and never moves out of its narrow range of emotions, chief among which is frustration (Laetitia, Vernon, Clara and Willoughby are all frustrated). He adds the further, fictive, unity that the book is seen largely from a single point of view, that of Clara. He does, however, allow us to know Sir Willoughby's thoughts: he transcribes them apparently quite straightforwardly and often without commentary. But the mind of the reader scrutinises them. In this way he allows us to make the same discoveries about Sir Willoughby as Clara does, by a means additional to, and to some extent independent of, hers. At times it seems scarcely believable that Sir Willoughby should fail to recognise his motives for what they are, so clearly does he state grossly selfish ideas to himself; but it is precisely the failure to take that final step to self-consciousness which involves self-criticism which makes Sir Willoughby what he is. By making us share Sir Willoughby's stream-of-consciousness, Meredith further suggests that we all think, quite lucidly, many more thoughts than we dare scrutinise.

His observation of the two principal characters is scrupulously exact. For example the deliberately uncharming account of the way Clara desperately annexes confidants: first Laetitia, then Vernon, then Mrs Mountstuart (it is important for our estimate of her that she only *seems* to have confided in Horace de Craye). This series of incidents is both a comic exaggeration of the conventional role of the confidante (a role found in French neo-classical *tragedy*) and a representation of the hysterical urge to be understood and justified which is common to most of us in emotional crises. This realism and inwardness (which reaffirms the emotional meaning of literary conventions) is seen also in the picture of Laetitia. It combines uneasily with the extremely formal dramatic structure of the last part of the book, in which all the devices of high comedy are deployed: the hidden listener, Crossjaye, who unintentionally hears Sir Willoughby's midnight proposal to Laetitia; the chapter headings from stage directions; the comic chorus of county ladies; the crowding of all the characters onto the stage for the scintillating untying of knots.

The delight of the book's conclusion (as well as its drop in intensity) comes because the solutions imposed derive from a more familiar literary world. Willoughby has been made to look ridiculous (to the reader, but not entirely to the other characters). His victories may be hollow, but they clothe his nakedness—and for him this preserves his identity, which is vested in appearances. (His favourite image of himself is as *le roi soleil.*) Clara has won her battle—but at the end of the book is a little withdrawn, so that she seems again just an ordinary young woman.

The sense of comic release at the end of the novel is in part a sense of release from the stringency of Meredith's comic vision. He said himself that the book contained 'only half myself'; the tart rationality of the scrutinising Comic Spirit cannot fully contain the emotional force of the characters. The comic imps are not our representatives. They come from a different world. They inhibit our involvement with the characters, but we are not like them. It is a situation akin to the fourth book of *Gulliver's Travels*: we cannot comfortably identify ourselves with either group. Comic imps and Houhyhynyms, however admirable, are ineffacably different from us. At times the primness of the narrative insistence on folly seems limited in the face of the characters' suffering, whether or not the suffering is self-imposed. We are not kept at the 'point fixe' of comedy: we move into the characters, then very far away, to where they seem like comic china ornaments caught in grotesque attitudes. The emotional energy of the book is such that at times the rigid comic form is almost shattered.

In his next novel, *The Tragic Comedians*, Meredith treats a similar story: an engagement broken by the woman and the man's frantic attempts to restore the relationship. This time his sources were in life not art and he was attempting to draw forth some meaningful pattern from an apparently arbitrary waste. Instead of suppressing the relationships as in *The Egoist*, in *The Tragic Comedians* he shows us the genuine and growing richness of love between a man and a woman (in history Ferdinand Lassalle and Helene von Dönniges) and the destruction of this love relationship through the pressures of society and through the weaknesses of the lovers themselves.

Meredith's sources were Helene von Racowitza's *Meine Beziehungen zu Ferdinand Lassalle* and J. M. Ludlow's article 'Ferdinand Lassalle, the German Social Democrat' in the *Fortnightly Review*.[14] His relation to his story is more complicated in *The Tragic Comedians* than in *The Egoist*. The facts are historical, and he is determined to present them as he knows them, without any fictional manipulation. But his interpretation of the facts differs from that of Frau von Racowitza so radically that his view of the events becomes a judgment on hers. He is involved in a dispute with the heroine. Equally, however, his view of Alvan (Lassalle), the hero, differs from that of J. M. Ludlow. Ludlow adopted a superficially Meredithian attitude of sound common sense towards Lassalle's pretensions, but Meredith sees that this is an inadequate response to Alvan's genuine if flawed nobility. Life and non-fictional literary sources become involved in a complicated interplay. Meredith undergoes a process of disillusionment with Clotilde, who was a real living woman, not merely a character of his imagination. The tragic strain is far more potent because the events really happened. Instead of creating an artefact designed specifically to figure forth the artist's ideas, Meredith is attempting to draw some instructive pattern out of a seemingly meaningless waste of talent and life. It must be remembered that Ferdinand Lassalle, the original of Alvan, was a politician of real importance, as influential in the Labour movement of his time as Marx himself. Meredith therefore has a situation artistically akin to Greek tragedy, in which the story is already known to the audience, who are assumed to have preconceptions about it. He wants to undermine the obvious meanings which others have assigned to the story.

He will accept it neither as a romantic Romeo-and-Juliet tragedy nor as a picture of vice leading to its own undoing. He shows with considerable irony how both Alvan and Clotilde refuse to recognise the weaknesses of their own natures: her craving to be dominated, which leads her to worship power instead of an individual, and his yearning for respectability and denial of his own capacity for violence. Alvan, Meredith insists, is not a self-inflated figure like Sir Willoughby. He is 'hugely man', and if he had also accepted his own animality he would not have been a prey for the comic spirit. Clotilde bears the brunt of Meredith's pursuit of Folly, but there is no simple division between hero and heroine. The heroine behaves in a conventionally laudable fashion in submitting to the wishes of her family, but she forms an unfavourable contrast with Clara in *The Egoist*, who pursues her will to escape with more energy than Clotilde can muster for her will to love.

True reason, it seems, cannot necessarily be equated with the conventional attitudes of society, although Meredith had written in the *Essay* that it was the first condition of sanity to believe that our civilisation is founded on common sense. In the *Essay* Meredith says of women that: 'Comedy is an exhibition of their battle with men, and that of men with them'. This battle is the root of both the novels, but in the comic *Egoist* Clara is victorious and keeps her integrity, whereas in *The Tragic Comedians* Clotilde's vacillation results in her self-destruction. By the end of the book she is incapable of feeling. In *The Tragic Comedians* the man is the centre of sympathy and by allowing us to sympathise primarily with the character who is striving for a fulfillment of love instead of with a character who is fleeing an intolerable love as in *The Egoist*, Meredith swings the balance of *The Tragic Comedians* decisively away from the appraising light of comedy towards a more generous sense of the tragic potential of life—a sense which persisted and grew through the works of his last years.

The Egoist is high comedy of the kind which 'refines even to pain'. Despite his belief in the power of reason, Meredith's own creative sympathy is usually given to passionate feeling. Clara is justified by her passionate revulsion against Sir Willoughby in which both mind and instincts play a part. The characters speak with grace and wit; they are allusive, urbane, epigrammatic, apparently articulate—but what they say nearly always serves as a foil to their urgent, often ugly feelings. Meredith sets up a fruitful tension between the poise of high comedy and the primitive emotions with which the characters are grappling. It is the abrasion between comedy and passion which makes the book both witty and poignant.

5

Diana of the Crossways
The Novelist in the Novel

IN *Diana of the Crossways* (1885) Meredith treats a theme particularly rich in self-expressive possibilities: making a novel about a novelist. Such writing involves self-scrutiny, and when, as in this book, the author's own aims and methods of composition are similar to those he ascribes to his character, it may act equally as self-criticism and *apologia*. By making his novelist a woman and an amateur Meredith sets her decisively and sufficiently apart from himself. At the same time he is able to suggest the particular stresses which beset the creatively intellectual woman in a society antagonistic to her claims: she may be obliged either to sacrifice her feminine nature or become enslaved by it. The central theme of the novel is the disparity between the awakened intellect and the slumbering sexual nature of his Diana-heroine; the movement of the work is seismographic, tracking deep emotional stirrings and irruptions which on the surface may seem disconnected. Diana's attempt to reconcile her individual identity with her inescapable instinctive being is the central concern of the book.

Meredith handled with a sophistication in advance of most of his contemporaries the confused relationship between self and identity suggested in the semantic closeness of self and selfishness, ego and egotism. The exploration of individual identity is a subject peculiarly appropriate to the novel, with its protracted timescape of experience for characters and reader alike. But the ethics of a pre-Freudian age meant that novelists approached it with mixed feelings, self being something to combat, not accept. George Eliot's novels pursue personality through a series of moral choices which pare away possibilities until the quintessential being is defined, and the criterion of judgment is finally whether the character is 'selfish' or 'unselfish'. We can contrast this with the feeling for fluidity of personality in a novel like *Women in Love*. Although Lawrence uses a traditional antithetical structure, comparing the development of two relationships, he emphasises how identity forms and re-forms rather than progresses. The assertion and discovery of self, rather than its subjugation, is for him the central positive value.

Meredith was sufficiently a Victorian to be troubled by the omnipresence of self but he was also fascinated by its disguises and its manifold expressions in action. The tension between these two attitudes at first hampered him but in *Beauchamp's Career* and *The Egoist* the conflict provides the energy of the action. In the later novels he more and more emphasises that it is not simply egoism which causes mischief but the refusal to recognise and accept one's own egoism—the refusal to acknowledge the disparate potentialities of one's identity, and the inconsequent-seeming dominance of varied characteristics at various times. In the course of his analytical explorations he largely abandons the notion of congruity of character—the idea of a coherent pattern of behaviour appropriate to a particular person which excludes a whole range of possible actions. In works such as *Diana of the Crossways* and *One of Our Conquerors* he suggests that a personality may express itself in actions showing widely various moral qualities, and that the traditional ethical hierarchy is inadequate as a guide for our response to individuality. At the same time, in these late books he places an unsentimental emphasis on the extent to which actions are determined by society. He sees the small amount of free expression attained by those most devoted to personal freedom, such as Diana Warwick or Victor Radnor,

Thus his later books are conceived in terms of complete societies and can legitimately be read, as Jack Lindsay reads them, as an attack on capitalist values.[1] Meredith, however, is always primarily concerned with individual responsibility.

He uses Diana's role as authoress and wit in two diverse ways. His examination of Diana's craftsmanship as a novelist allows him to present in dramatic form many of the critical problems which beset him in the eighteen-eighties: the relationship between the 'realistic' novel and the revived fashion for the 'romance'; the problem of establishing a style for the novel which can encompass wit, intricacy, and the author's idiosyncratic consciousness without entirely abandoning the common medium of contemporary language; and the responsibility of the novelist towards his society and towards the models in life on whom he draws for his art. His examination of Diana's books and their interplay with her own life enables him to represent creatively many of the propositions about the art of the novel which he puts forward in his opening chapter. Her response as an artist to her readers and critics allows him to show the relationship between writer and reader in action—that relationship which troubled him throughout his career and which in his own work contained always a large element of antagonism. Even more, Meredith uses the relationship between her life and her novels to show the variable consciousness within even an articulate and honest person. Objectively, she understands; in her own conduct, she is blind.

Meredith is particularly successful in his portrayals of articulate people: and he repeatedly shows that intelligence does not automatically bestow self-knowledge. The act of analysis is in itself an act of dramatisation. It is set apart from the amorphousness of continuous being. In Meredith's own creativity there is a close relationship between autobiography and art—and art functions particularly as self-admonition. Unlike Diana, he habitually handles autobiographical elements in his work with harsh self-consciousness.

Within this novel there are several minor autobiographical strands which suggest Meredith's repudiating bitterness by the very slightness of their treatment in the work: the portrait of the young poet, Arthur Rhodes, a lawyer's clerk, draws mordantly on Meredith's own early circumstances; the scene of Sir Lukin's agony of remorse when his wife is undergoing surgery for cancer was written, disturbingly, when Meredith's own wife was dying, or perhaps had already died, of the disease. Diana, discussing the irony of her situation after the loss of Dacier, refers to an incident from Meredith's life: 'A friend of Dada's waited patiently for a small fortune, and when it arrived, he was a worn-out man, just assisted to go decently to his grave' (xxxviii; 431).[2] Meredith himself had waited long for a legacy from an old imbecile aunt, which, he told Photiadès, made possible the writing of his late books beginning with *Diana*. There is here (concealed below the surface of the novel) a hidden emotional acknowledgment which is the converse, rather than the opposite, of Diana's failure to recognise the personal implications of her fiction. She can use Percy Dacier as the hero of her book *The Young Minister of State* without recognising that the portrait expresses her hidden love for him; she can use her faithful friend, Redworth, as the model for the worshipper of an opera-singer without recognising his restrained passion for her—and without seeing that the subtlety and intensity of his feeling contradicts her fictional portrait of him as an unimaginative Briton.[3]

Diana acts as mouthpiece for Meredith's belief in the need for fuller realism in the novel, a realism which will avoid the sentimental simplification of human behaviour but which will reach beyond the determinism of the French Naturalists. The 'Naturalists', Diana (and Meredith) consider, do not recognise the extent to which individual consciousness, 'mind', affects our nature. To them, we are wholly composed of appetites.

> 'I wonder whether the world is as bad as a certain class of writers tell us!' she sighed in weariness, and mused on their soundings and probings of poor humanity, which the world accepts for the very bottom-truth if their dredge brings up sheer refuse of the abominable. The world imagines those to be at our nature's depths who are impudent enough to expose its muddy shallows. She was in the mood for such a kind of writing: she could have started on it at once but that the theme was wanting; and it may count on popularity, a great repute for penetration. It is true of its kind, though the dredging of nature is the miry form of art. When it flourishes we may be assured we have been over-enamelling the higher forms. (xxiv; 274–5)

Diana of the Crossways is Meredith's own fullest attempt at psychological realism though it does not attempt the broad social spectrum of his next novel, *One of Our Conquerors*. It occurs at a crucial stage in his career. Oscar Wilde said of Meredith's work in 'The Decay of Lying' (1889) that 'whatever he is, he is not a realist'.

> Or rather I would say that he is a child of realism who is not on speaking terms with his father. By deliberate choice he has made himself a romanticist. He has refused to bow the knee to Baal, and after all, even if the man's fine spirit did not revolt against the noisy assertions of realism, his style would be quite sufficient of itself to keep life at a respectful distance.[4]

Kenneth Graham's study of contemporary criticism of the novel has brought sharply into focus the intensity and scope of the critical debate in the eighteen-eighties between the 'realistic' novel and the 'romance'.[5] Robert Louis Stevenson, one of Meredith's earliest and warmest admirers, combined a concern with craftsmanship in the novel with a taste for the exotic and sensational in setting and incident. To the writers of 'romance' Meredith, after *Harry Richmond*, may have seemed a model—but he himself despised both 'rose-pink and dirty drab' and sought to be 'veraciously historical, honestly transcriptive'. His idea of history and transcription had little to do with documentation. (*Diana* is based on historical incidents of 1836 and 1845; she hears Chopin play in London (xviii; 204); her friend Redworth is speculating in railway shares; the Diarists who discuss her in the first chapter are 'beginning with the second quarter of our Century'; the political arguments are concerned with the union of Ireland and England; references to the Regent and to Chartism in a context of dinner-party conversation are simply coins of talk.)

'The brainstuff of fiction is internal history', Meredith writes: and he first presents Diana to us through her reported conversation and through the Diarist's comments on her personal ebullience. He wishes to replace 'the barren aspects' of pink and drab with 'a pure decency in the place of sham; real flesh; a soul born active, wind-beaten, but ascending'. Nature 'in the flesh' he says is 'flower-like, yet not too decoratively a flower; you must have her with the stem, the thorns, the roots, and the fat bedding of roses' (i; 16). This is his idea of 'philosophy'—not a coherent abstracting argument but an acceptance of man's unity and of his relationship to the natural world through the communicating intelligence.

The book's method is cerebral and symbolic; Diana attempts to live in the mind alone, acting as Princess Egeria to Percy Dacier (and forgetting that Egeria was not only the adviser but the mistress of Numa). Like his heroine, Meredith delights in the play of the intellect, but the book also explores its dangers, in particular the danger that intellect may be falsely identified with reason and give an illusion of emotional control. Through the story of Diana Merion, and equally through his own artistic relationship to his creation, Meredith explored the problem of how to respond intelligently and yet wholly to the flux of experience and personality. He abandoned the detached control of comedy and the heightened absolutes of romance. He bypassed the finality of tragedy.

The basis of his plot was drawn from history. It is the method he used also in *The Tragic Comedians*, his preceding novel, and suggests a need to engage with things as they are, instead of inventing a malleable story which is shaped only by the will of the writer. This need to grapple with the actual which had been growing in Meredith since the writing of *Beauchamp's Career*, was reinforced by the agonising experience of his wife's death. It found expression in the poems of *A Faith on Trial*, and is the emotional basis of the artist's longing for a richer realism.

Realism usually suggests a concern with the structure of society. Realism in this novel consists in the degree of complexity with which the individual consciousness is explored. By making this the centre, and by setting his story at least forty years back in time, Meredith avoided the study of contemporary social issues, except those which he chose to use, such as the problem of Union between England and Ireland. This narrows the import of the work: historical figures and issues are here peripheral, of significance only in their bearing on Diana's story. True, Diana says: 'Ah! the mind. We imagine it free. The House and the country are the sentient frame governing the mind of the politician more than his ideas. He cannot think independently of them: nor I of my natural anatomy (xxii; 251). But she does not recognise that she is governed by politics and society as well as by her 'natural anatomy'. To her, politics is a personal affair—a coin in intellectual and amatory exchange. In her relationship first to Lord Dannisburgh and then to his nephew Percy Dacier she has been gratified by her special knowledge of the affairs of state, but she does not grasp that these have significance and effect outside her own circle of privilege. The problem is to know how far beyond his heroine Meredith saw in this matter. The way he treats Diana's experience after she has betrayed a political secret suggests that the social implications of her action did not much interest him. Perhaps he was unsatisfied with the relationship between the individual and society that he suggests in *Diana*, for his next, important novel, *One of Our Conquerors*, is his fullest study of the social order of contemporary England. But Meredith is always interested by the individual's will towards *freedom* rather than by responsibility within society. And the effects of society upon the individual are seen in terms of 'social' prejudice, rather than in broader economic or sociological terms. Both Diana and Victor Radnor are in a sense *entrepreneurs*: she a political hostess and novelist, he a manipulator of money in the City.

The historical episodes on which Meredith based the story concern Mrs Caroline Norton. Writing to R. L. Stevenson in 1884 Meredith says that the work is 'partly modelled upon Mrs Norton. But this is between ourselves. I have had to endow her with brains, and make them evidence to the discerning. I think she lives' (*Letters*, ii, 355). In 1836 Mrs Caroline Norton, novelist and granddaughter of Sheridan, was involved in a 'criminal conversation' suit brought by her husband against the Whig Prime Minister, Lord Melbourne. The evidence was trivial and obviously corrupt; the case was dismissed. In 1845 she was reputed to have informed the editor of *The Times* of Sir Robert Peel's decision to repeal the Corn Laws—a secret which had been confided to her by an admirer, Sidney Herbert. Meredith met Mrs Norton at the Duff Gordons in the eighteen-fifties, and her novel *Lost and Saved* was reviewed by Justin McCarthy in the *Westminster Review* (July 1864) alongside *Richard Feverel* and *Sandra Belloni*. Meredith thus had some slight acquaintance with the original of his heroine. In this novel he uses all the elements in Mrs Norton's public career, though in later editions of the work he inserted a somewhat elliptical disclaimer. 'A lady of high distinction for wit and beauty, the daughter of an illustrious Irish House, came under the shadow of a calumny. It has latterly been examined and exposed as baseless. The story of Diana of the Crossways is to be read as fiction.' This makes no attempt to deny that

Diana is based on Mrs Norton. A list of '*Comediettas in Narrative*' in the 'Dramatic Dialogue' Portfolio includes 'Diana (Mrs N. & Lord M.)'. Among other items in the same list are 'Autobiography (with Contrivance Tom)', 'The Case of General Ople and Lady Cass', 'The Egoist—(Willoughby Patterne)', 'The Amazing Marriage (Gossip as Chorus)' and 'Adiante'. If these are projected works (as appears from the variant versions of the published titles) it would seem that he had thought of the topics for several of his late novels, including *Diana*, some time before 1870 when the 'Autobiography (with Contrivance Tom)' had grown into *The Adventures of Harry Richmond*.

When he came to write *Diana of the Crossways* (by 7 December 1881 he was 'in harness'), he created a personality which encompasses a larger diversity of feeling than is implicit in the 'facts' of Mrs Norton's career. In *The Tragic Comedians* he wanted to disarrange the trite moral patterns which had been imposed on a 'well-known story'. In *Diana* he sought a coherent reading of personality which could encompass Diana's violently contrasted actions. Moreover, the novel marked a summation of his concern with the 'celtic' strain in personality, which became both an idealising means of separating himself from the mass of English people (with their heavier 'Teuton' blood), and a justification of his heightened language. Writing to Arthur Meredith in 1881, after their long estrangement, he attempts to establish contact through an interest in his son's writing on language and says:

I fancy still that you are in danger of overlooking the large admixture of Celtic blood in the English race. Irish and Cambrian have a portion of them under that banner.— . . . As far as I observe them, the heart of the nation is Teuton and moral, and therewith intellectually obtuse, next to speechless. It has, however, a shifty element, and a poetic: and this tells again for you, that the poetic, seeming to come from our Celtic blood, flies at once to the well-springs of the tongue whenever it is in need of vital imagery.' (*Letters*, i, 322)

The theme of England and Ireland and their need for union, became a type for morality and imagination, realism and romance—and represented the clash within his own artistic personality. The theme was developed in terms of a love-affair in the unfinished novel *Celt and Saxon* (or 'Adiante' as it is called in the notebooks and portfolios). In that novel his declared theme is 'an ideal of country, of Great Britain . . . to the taste of Celt and Saxon in common':

> The theme is chosen and must be treated as a piper involved in his virtue conceives it: that is, realistically; not with Bull's notion of the realism of the butcher's shop and the pendent legs of mutton and blocks of beef painted raw and glaring in their streaks, but with the realism of the active brain and heart conjoined.' (xvi; 243–4)

In *Diana of the Crossways* he shows (more tellingly than in this bombastic declaration) how his heroine achieves 'the active brain and heart conjoined'. She is 'shifty' and 'poetic'; Redworth, the man she finally marries, is the moral Teuton Englishman—but the course of the book shows that he is not without imagination.

In Meredith's version of the story Diana Merion, a young, witty and handsome Irish beauty of little fortune, makes a precipitate and ill-assorted marriage with a formal Englishman, Mr Warwick. The marriage comes about partly because she associates him with Crossways, the home of her late beloved father, partly because her friend's husband has made advances to her (another, similar early episode is described only near the end of the novel). After her marriage she forms a close friendship with an elderly statesman, Lord Dannisburgh, who has given her husband an appointment. Her husband sues for divorce on the grounds of misconduct but loses the case. Husband and wife separate. A few months later Diana begins an intense and intellectual friendship with Percy Dacier, Lord Dannisburgh's nephew, who has come to value her with new admiration after seeing her at his uncle's death-bed. This friendship, always hovering on the brink of fully-acknowledged passion, almost reaches fruition when they plan to leave for Europe together, but Diana is deflected by the news of her friend Emma Dunstane's illness. The friendship between Diana and Dacier comes finally and abruptly to an end when Diana, in a state of emotional shock, sells an important political secret entrusted to her by Dacier. He immediately proposes to another woman. In the last section of the book we are shown the stages by which she moves to marriage with her faithful admirer, Redworth.

Diana is first presented to the reader at a ball in Dublin, where, despite the men who are eager for her attention, her relationship to her friend, Emma Dunstane, is shown as emotionally dominant. This relationship (which is Meredith's most extensive fictitious addition to his source material) is crucial throughout the book and invokes Diana's only sustained feeling. In it Meredith attempts to present a reality which lives behind the literary cliché of 'intimate female friendship'. Diana's intellect and emotions are unified only in her relationship with Emma. In her relationships with men sexual stress fragments her responsiveness. The ardour of the relationship might tempt a modern reader to think it lesbian in impulse, just as the relationship between Merthyr Powys and his sister in *Sandra Belloni* could be called incestuous: but Meredith undercuts such labels. As he says approvingly of Nesta in *One of our Conquerors*, 'Her vision of the reality of things was without written titles, to put the stamp of the world on it.' He presents relationships as they exist to the people involved, not as they might appear to a diagrammatising world. *Diana of the Crossways* shows how spectators misunderstand the real nature of relationships; but Meredith does not suggest that they are fully understood by those involved and he shows that any relationship is always in a state of flux. Within the sustained friendship of the two women there are unspoken periods of estrangement; and Diana, for all her intelligence, avoids understanding the implications of Redworth's friendship for her or her own feelings for Dacier. In this novel, it is only when a relationship is over that analysis of it can be performed.

Throughout, however, Meredith suggests the qualities of the relationships through symbol and metaphor. In contrast to *The Egoist*, where the analogies are used to support the reader in his expectations, he uses his more typical method of inverting or diverting the expected course of allusions. It is essentially sceptical, bringing quiet assumptions into question anew, just as his language uses puns and kennings to revivify dead metaphors. Here the method is itself an object of mild satire. Emma Dunstane speaks of it as 'estate-agent's language': 'That plush of speech haunts all efforts to swell and illuminate citizen prose to a princely poetic' (iv; 45).

More than in any other of Meredith's novels, the implications of the story are expressed through references to myth. *Diana of the Crossways* is the first novel for many years in which Meredith is treating directly a topic concerned with sexual morality. He had been dismayed by his early experience with *Richard Feverel*, which Mudie's circulating library withdrew after complaints of the Bella Mount–Richard seduction scene. In that early novel he represents and seeks to rouse sexual feeling through the excitement of the woman's mannish role-playing. His novels of the eighteen-seventies describe the prelude of choice before marriage: in his last four novels he turns to the subject of love-relationships outside and after marriage.

Meredith is now concerned with graver and more equal loves than that between the boyish Richard and the practised older woman. In *Diana*, *One of Our Conquerors*, *Lord Ormont and his Aminta* and *The Amazing Marriage*—and particularly in the first three—he wishes to convey adult experience with all the closeness and truth of which he is capable. His readers must know that Diana has withdrawn physically from her husband after they have begun to quarrel and that this is what spurs him to believe that she is having an affair with Lord Dannisburgh—but their attention must not be fastened on this fact too directly. The covert obsession of Diana's love for Dacier must be shown without her seeming to understand it. The sexual force in Redworth must be suggested, in order to offset the public picture of him as a sensible, careful businessman and member of parliament unlikely to be a match for Diana's temperament.

Meredith creates a language to communicate sexual experience by adapting the myths of Diana. In this, of course, he is not alone among Victorian writers. Classical mythology provided a perfect method of rendering sexual meaning while preserving an effect of respectable objectivity; its obscurity for modern readers means that classical allusions which are really organic and suggestive are dismissed as merely ornamental and static.

In *Diana of the Crossways* the heroine's name has many aspects. Diana is the goddess of chastity and of hunting; she is the moon goddess; and she protects women in childbirth. Diana of the woods is worshipped in groves, but Diana of the crossroads is Hecate. Diana warns Dacier: 'My Christian name! It is Pagan. In one sphere I am Hecate. Remember that' (xxii; 253). To the social world about her, Diana seems a predatory woman, pursuing men of fortune and ambition. This is Lady Wathin's view (her hostility begins because at a dinner-party she doesn't understand a joke about Hero and Leander and Diana's guard dog). The image of the hunt and of Diana as the chaste huntress is fragmented and diffused throughout the book. Diana, traditionally the huntress, is here the hunted. In the first chapter the narrator warns us against the hunting instinct: civilisation consists in holding back. Diana's name seems a mockery to those who distrust her, but we gradually perceive that her troubles arise from her unawakenedness and her sexual repugnance. Yet in believing herself to be cold, Diana, also, basically misunderstands her own nature. She responds to old men who remind her of her dead father. Lord Larrian, her first platonic elderly admirer, gives her a guard dog so that she can walk freely in London without fear of molestation. Her marriage with Mr Warwick is prompted by sexual fear—she has been 'worshipped in a grove' by Sir Lukin—and by her need for the emotional security suggested by Crossways, the house in which they are to live. Crossways represents stability to Diana because it has been her father's house: but it also marks the moments of decision and choice in her life. She says of her marriage: 'We walked a dozen steps in stupefied union, and hit upon crossways' (xiv; 156). After she has left her husband she goes to Crossways on her way to France—and it is there that Redworth finds her and hands her Emma Dunstane's letter which persuades her to stay in England. 'I am always at crossways, and he rescues me', Diana says later (xxvii; 308). Crossways is a benign place, not a temple of Hecate; but it is also the psychological meeting point of 'the woman of two natures'—Diana's own embittered evaluation of herself after her betrayal of Dacier. The multiple possibilities of her personality are suggested by the number of names used by her and of her: Diana Merion; Antonia as pen-name; Tony as love-name (her use of a man's name for intimacy is striking); Mrs Warwick; Princess Egeria. The Hecate of crossroad-images traditionally had three faces.

The chastity and coldness of the goddess, Diana, represent intimate levels of Diana Warwick's experience invisible to the world about her. The images of hunting and of nakedness are used with particular force in the relationship of Diana and Dacier—that seemingly intellectual affair. In this book men are the hunters. But Diana recognises that 'our weakness is the swiftest dog to hunt us; we cannot escape it'. Redworth is distinguished from all the other men because he refuses to pursue (and in the last section of the book he becomes sun god to Diana's moon goddess). Dacier, whose brother is a 'common Nimrod', believes himself free of the crude impulse of the hunting male:

Was it not, on the contrary, a serious pursuit of the secret of a woman's character? ... Ordinary women and their characters might set to work to get what relationship and likeness they could. They had no secret to allure. This one had: she had the secret of lake waters under rock, unfathomable in limpidness. He could not think of her without shooting at nature, and nature's very sweetest and subtlest, for comparisons. As to her sex, his active man's contempt of the petticoated secret attractive to boys and graylings, made him believe that in her he hunted the mind and the spirit: perchance a double mind, a twilighted spirit; but not a mere woman. (xvi; 177)

These meditations are immediately followed by a scene glimmering with allusions to the Diana–Actaeon legend. They are pointed up by the commentary in a way that makes it rather heavily clear that we need to understand the allusions. Dacier rising at dawn to bathe in a mountain stream comes upon Diana standing unaware beside the pool.

They have that whisper and waving of secrecy in secret scenery; they beckon to the bath; and they conjure classic visions of the pudency of the Goddess irate or unsighted. The semi-mythological state of mind, built of old images and favouring haunts, was known to Dacier. The name of Diana, playing vaguely on his consciousness, helped to it. He had no definite thought of the mortal woman when the highest grass-roll near the rock gave him view of a bowered source and of a pool under a chain of cascades, bounded by polished shelves and slabs. The very spot for him, he decided at the first peep; and at the second, with fingers instinctively loosening his waistcoat-buttons for a commencement, he shouldered round and strolled away, though not at a rapid pace, nor far before he halted.

That it could be no other than she, the figure he had seen standing beside the pool, he was sure. Why had he turned? (xvi; 180)

This meeting is the long-unacknowledged beginning of their love—a love which ends in the near destruction not of

Dacier but Diana. The correspondences are fleeting and suggested as much by contrast as parallel—here it is Dacier not Diana who is about to bathe. He, the course of the book implies, is without passion whereas Diana is not yet wakened to warmth.

The image of being stripped bare by hunters becomes an image of Diana's fear of confronting her inmost self. She dreads self-exposure more than the loss of her reputation. After separating from her husband she says to herself. 'Wherever I go now, in all weathers, I am perfectly naked!' (xi; 120). But this is not fully so; she feels herself exposed in society but she retains areas of secrecy veiled even from herself; the narrator comments that she 'was less indiscreet in her thoughts than in her acts'. Meredith scrutinises her half-suppressed awareness that, though innocent of her husband's accusations, she is not without blame for the breakdown of her marriage: 'his wretched jealousy had ruined her' but the 'secret high tribunal within her bosom' 'pronounced him just pardonable' because he could only conceive one bad reason for her 'putting the sword between their marriage tie when they stood as one, because a quarrelling couple could not in honour play the embracing' (xv; 162).

Meredith does not suggest that his heroine is unusually blind ('The black dog of consciousness declines to be shaken off', says Diana (xviii; 205)). He shows indeed that she is seized with swift and unavoidable intuitions into her own state, and he endows her with a heightened 'celtic' sensibility. But heightened consciousness imposes the need for disguises. The inner eye is so acute that perceptions and covering fantasies proliferate with equal energy. This process is at work in Diana's recurring memory of the scene at Lugano when she met Percy Dacier in the dawn. At first the image is a touchstone, an assurance of her own heart-wholeness and purity of feeling. Gradually, however, she begins to suspect her own eagerness to remember that dawn.

Finally she brings herself to acknowledge that it was after her meeting with Dacier that she experienced the access of lyrical joy which she believed to spring from her new freedom of identity; Meredith adds his own combative commentary on the 'fiction of a perfect ignorant innocence'; he represents her half-perceptions through the imagery of a bird on a cliff face which 'takes short flights to the troubled waters'.

> If at intervals her soul flew out like lightning from the rift (a mere shot of involuntary fancy, it seemed to her), the suspicion of instability made her draw on her treasury of impressions of the mornings at Lugano—her loftiest, purest, dearest; and these reinforced her. She did not ask herself why she should have to seek them for aid. In other respects her mind was alert and held no sly covers . . . (xxi; 244)

Mythology becomes a means of endorsing the *stature* of his heroine while questioning her aspirations. The many-aspected Goddess is a higher corollary for Diana Warwick's various identity. At the end of the book she is Lucina—she is expecting a child. Such intricacy can seem frivolous or cold if its virtuosity is greater than its implications, but Meredith diffuses the mythological references with surprising delicacy through the sinuous movement of the book. He is claiming to be a historian, not a myth-maker; and myth, with its simplification and mystification of human material, would seem to be at the opposite end of the spectrum from 'realism', here interpreted as the intense scrutiny of the individual experience. He invokes and fragments mythological material in his representation of 'Reality's infinite sweetness'. He offsets the generality of known 'facts' (the story of Mrs Norton) by invoking another, idealising, generality—that of myth, with its suggestive imaging of the psyche's wishes.

'The art of the pen (we write on darkness) is to rouse the inward vision', says Diana, and Meredith struggles in this book to render the full reality of an individual to the imagination of the reader. He succeeded in creating a vivid character who existed for his contemporaries beyond the bounds of the novel: Yeats, two days after his first meeting with Maud Gonne in 1889, wrote that she is a 'kind of Diana of the Crossways'.[6] For Meredith himself she existed so entirely that he continued to argue about her behaviour (offering in correspondence several years later arguments not explicit in the book itself).[7] But this full realisation of Diana makes Meredith partisan rather than chronicler. He sees beyond her ego but, even more, he *participates* in it. And this relationship towards his heroine defines the limits of his realism. Despite his insistence on his heroine's failures of intelligence and emotion, Meredith as artist and commentator is aligned with her. Diana, in her third novel, *The Cantatrice*, writes in a style which parallels Meredith's method in the book:

No clever transcripts of the dialogue of the day occurred; no hair-breadth 'scapes, perils by sea and land, heroisms of the hero, fine shrieks of the heroine; no set scenes of catching pathos and humour; no distinguishable points of social satire—equivalent to a smacking of the public on the chaps, which excites it to grin with keen discernment of the author's intention. She did not appeal to the senses nor to a superficial discernment. So she had the anticipatory sense of its failure; and she wrote her best, in perverseness; of course she wrote slowly; she wrote more and more realistically of the characters and the downright human emotions, less of the wooden supernumeraries of her story, labelled for broad guffaw or deluge tears—the grappling natural links between our public and an author. (xxiii; 263)

We can hear the tone of the wearied publisher's reader here; Meredith is describing the taste of his own audience, as much as of the eighteen thirties or forties. Meredith, in *Diana*, wrote 'more and more realistically of the characters and the downright human emotions' but only for certain favoured characters. Some, to avoid emotional complexities, he stiffens into 'wooden supernumeraries'. He does not, for instance, give any glimpse of Mr Warwick, Diana's husband, or of his view of the marriage. Warwick exists only as ogre or pathetic wreck, offstage. His individuality is allowed no expression: this is Meredith's method of insisting that he *has* no individuality—and hence no rights. This harsh artistic annihilation has perturbing parallels with Sir Willoughby's method of abolishing those who displease him. Meredith imputes rigour to Mr Warwick and then uses this to exclude him from our consideration.

The problems of a realism vested exclusively in the individual consciousness and not expressing itself also in terms of society arise in a more conspicuous form in the relationship between Dacier and Diana. How can the writer represent with equal richness the inner worlds of two undeclared lovers without either a false suggestion of complete mutual understanding or a tendentious absorption in one consciousness? Meredith elaborately charts the growth of their love. He shows Dacier's growing respect for Diana's identity and he tracks the intricate strategies of the subconscious in their shifting relationship.

We can see the interplay of actions and rationalisations very clearly in the episode of their abortive elopement. The elopement is prevented at the last moment by the news that Emma Dunstane is about to undergo a critical operation. Diana impetuously sets out for her country home, leaving Dacier, waiting for her at Victoria Station, feeling more and more ridiculous. Their decision has been approvingly presented as a fully weighed offering of themselves; but Diana's act of friendship is equally warmly presented. It expresses the deepest commitments of her nature, which are to affection, rather than to sexual love. Dacier's view of events is dramatised in the scene at Victoria but the reader's knowledge of Diana's real reason for not coming makes his embittered comments on her fickleness seem paltry.

The episode is deeply unsatisfactory because it raises and avoids so many possibilities. Our responses as readers are manipulated by Redworth's role as messenger (he has already saved Diana once from the disastrous error of flight to France); by the superiority of our knowledge over that of

Dacier; by the dramatic scene of Sir Lukin's remorse as he waits for the outcome of the operation. In these ways our attention is deflected from the *possibility* of the elopement; its impossibility springs from sources outside the psychological realism of the book and to some extent running counter to them. Meredith cannot as yet permit it to happen. (In his next novel, *Lord Ormont and his Aminta*, it finally takes place.) It cannot happen partly because it might alienate readers from Diana's cause before the crucial historical incidents which are to be the pivot of the book; partly because of the author's lack of affection for Dacier and his possessiveness towards his heroine. It takes all Meredith's skill to drive the story back from the course of elopement on which it is energetically set. The lovers' loss of purpose once the occasion is gone by is convincingly presented. More unexpectedly, we are shown that their secret love remains unchanged (and, by a further twist, thus begins to atrophy).

While presenting Diana's actions and consciousness with complete truthfulness, Meredith cannot bear to allow any loss of sympathy for her. This involves him in turgid and otiose *explanations* of what has been presented through image and action. The dense presentation, the scrupulous analysis determined by the author's endorsement of the heroine, makes the book laborious reading at times.

Meredith *shows* much that is original and daring about emotional stress and suggests new attitudes to the concept of 'congruity' of character in fiction. For example, after her betrayal of Dacier, Diana regresses, through a state of inertia, to unthinking infancy, then to querulous childishness when presented with emotional responsibility. She plays like an adolescent girl with young Arthur Rhodes, feeding on his adoration, and gradually emerges into an acceptance of womanhood in response to Redworth's ardent wooing, while still continuing to insist defensively that it is all very humdrum. This record of emotional illness and recovery is remarkably honest and intransigent.

Thus the *action* of the book makes understandable Diana's betrayal of Dacier while the opinions of Diana and others deliberately blur clear emotional sources. Diana, who thinks herself a cold intellect, enacts an inescapable pattern of impulsive and often disastrous action under emotional stress: her marriage to Warwick is the first clear instance. Her betrayal of Dacier shows the same forces at work. Sexual dread, a feeling of being diminished into an object, in both cases precipitate her into wild action. In our experience as readers, however, the two instances are not parallel: the first occurs so early in the book that it simply reveals to us a new aspect of a little known heroine: the reader moreover, knows more of her reasons than do her friends. Her betrayal of Dacier, however, shocks us as we are shocked in real life at realising anew the irremovable limits of intimacy. The artistic problem arises *not* because Diana's actions are 'incongruous' but because the novelist's commentary exculpates her even while Diana feels herself to blame. Chapter-headings such as 'In which it is darkly seen how the criminal's judge may be love's criminal' shift the blame to Dacier too easily.

Meredith had considerable trouble with writing the scenes preceding Diana's journey to the newspaper offices of Mr Tonans and her offer to sell the political secret. He revised and rewrote extensively. The final draft (in the Morgan library) shows that the scenes *after* the betrayal, when Dacier reads the article and confronts Diana, survive from an earlier version and come through unaltered into the first edition. But the section I am here discussing underwent an extra revision at a late stage. (The manuscript runs consecutively to page 779; the next page is numbered by Meredith 779–731; thereafter the numbering runs 732 to the end of the book, 987.) The fragmentary draft in the Huntington Library gives an earlier version of the scene between Diana and Dacier at night; and the draft at Yale makes more of Diana's need and her rapacity for money, which is an element in the betrayal. It shows how far she used Redworth to get money; and it more generously expresses the extent to which Dacier told her political secrets as the only means of expressing his love: 'Love being forbidden music, love could be implied in his absolute confidingness' (Yale MS 666) and 'Not less generous than she, he gave her his whole mind, every secret, in return for her fair fame: a sacrifice to be obliterated when she pleased' (Yale MS 691).

In the final version Meredith arranges the narrative sequence thus: After a 'brilliant' dinner party Diana sits down to composition. She is working on *The Man of Two Minds* and writing a scene which forms an unconscious commentary on her own view of her relationship with Dacier: the hero 'must induce the lady to school herself to his ideal' while she 'will drink any quantity of idealisation as long as it stems from a full acceptance of her acknowledged qualities' (xxxi; 360). Dacier unexpectedly returns near midnight. He comes laden with a political secret. Her enthusiasm and admiration excite him and he embraces her. Her *first* response is alarm because this will make it impossible for her to receive him freely (she is a married woman separated from an ailing husband). She fends him off by returning to political conversation until, after several pages of dialogue in which Dacier's urgent pleading contrasts with Diana's apparent coolness, the narrator intervenes to interpret:

> She cooled him further with eulogies of the chevaleresque manner of speaking which young Mr Rhodes could assume; till for very wrath of blood—not jealousy: he had none of any man, with her; and not passion; the little he had was a fitful gust—he punished her coldness by taking what hastily could be gathered. (xxxi; 365)

Her apparent restraint and coldness is here contrasted with the inner coldness of Dacier: but Dacier's coldness is ascribed rather than presented in the scene. After he has left, the effect on Diana of his embrace becomes clear. She is appalled: not because of the conventional view that a woman is 'degraded' by her lover using her against her will, but because she is finally unmasked to herself. She sees those inner recesses of her being which she has obstinately veiled; she now knows her own sexual responsiveness and the full meaning of her past actions:

> Something that was pressing her low, she knew not how, and left it unquestioned, incited her to exaggerate the indignity her pride had suffered. She was a dethroned woman. Deeper within, an unmasked actress, she said. Oh, she forgave him! But clearly he took her for the same as other women consenting to receive a privileged visitor. And sounding herself to the soul, was she so magnificently better? Her face flamed. She hugged her arms at her breast to quiet the beating, and dropped them when she surprised herself embracing the memory. (xxxii; 370)

Her nature is more passionate than Dacier's. She is a married woman who found no pleasure in her marriage and withdrew sexually from her husband as soon as they began to quarrel: she has fatally believed herself rational, intellectual and cold. This self-discovery and the knowledge that her last bulwark of independence is mundanely threatened by lack of money combine to drive her into a cold delirium. Mr Tonans, the newspaper editor, has told her that she is cut off from the centre of affairs: she sees an opportunity to re-establish herself as a Princess Egeria, an independent adviser, financially and emotionally. She drives with her maid to the newspaper offices and in an interview (which we are not shown) hands the secret to Tonans. It is action without foreseen consequence. The sparse, thin presentation of the drive and the crucial betrayal has a dramatic relevance. To Diana herself the incident has lost its implications—it exists only in surface meaning. She observes people passing the carriage window; she is interested by her visit to the newspaper-office. The reader is in the position of Danvers, the maid, who sits outside and knows little—and this psychologically is Diana's own position. Action simplifies; here it annihilates consciousness.

Meredith records these scenes with dramatic bareness. The artistic problem of the relationship of author to heroine becomes acute again only when the heroine is seen in relationship to other people. He is obliged to blacken Dacier in order to excuse Diana. The two succeeding chapters are ostensibly presented through Dacier's consciousness, but this consciousness is hostilely observed and reduced. And Diana's confession and gradual realisation of the meaning of what she has done are rapidly followed by the cruelly funny scene in which Dacier offers his hand in marriage to Miss Constance Asper, the snow-white high-church heiress his family want him to marry. This girl is 'the idol woman of imperishable type, who is never for a twinkling the prey of the blood'. She is the 'heroine of romance': the fair good heroine against the dark passionate one, and, as in romance, she comes 'finally to her time of triumph' (chapter heading, xxxv).

The antithesis between the heroine of romance and of reality had been used in a suppressed section of the first chapter (present in the Morgan Library final draft): Meredith contrasts the novel-heroines of the period he is describing with the women revealed by Diarists:

> For it is not the same as listening to her novelists. They, the most resolutely realistic of them, do soften the picture. They dare present to us the reeking male, haply the female scamp; their ladies, and above all their heroines, are tricked to pass approved through the rose-pink Court-chambers of posterity. A Diarist's heroine, on the other hand, a lady, young, beautiful, moving in the choicer circles, and not so very remote from us, confounds an impertinent in language approaching to salted midwife. . . . Mrs. M. Jackson Holdernesse (Records of a Long Life) tells the tale; she tells it baldly; and we are startled, we try to smile; an effort that dies in sickliness. Not such were the Sophias, the Amelias, the decorous Emmas, we have worshipped as the prize-women of their age! (MS 29)

Diana is a woman who (though not guilty as the world believes) is not innocent: she is complex and vital. Dacier, thinking back upon her after the break between them, describes her as the 'heroine of romance', but the narrator intervenes:

> He said to himself, with little intuition of the popular taste: She wouldn't be a bad heroine of Romance! He said it derisively of the Romantic. But the right worshipful heroine of Romance was the front-face female picture he had won for his walls. Poor Diana was the flecked heroine of Reality: not always the same; not impeccable; not an ignorant-innocent, nor a guileless: good under good leading; devoted to death in a grave crisis; often wrestling with her terrestrial nature nobly; and a growing soul . . . (xxxv; 399)

This impassioned vindication is followed by a passage in which Meredith dismisses the notion that the heroine's distress is caused by any villain:

> Your fair one of Romance cannot suffer a mishap without a plotting villain, perchance many of them, to wreak the dread iniquity: she cannot move without him; she is the marble block, and if she is to have a feature, he is the sculptor; she depends on him for life, and her human history at least is married to him far more than to the rescuing lover. (xxxv; 399–400)

Meredith records the diffused eddying of feeling and action; he insists on the protracted growth of relationships; he eschews the heightened scene; he rejects novel conventions which tighten and simplify the deviousness of human feeling. He shows also the folly of believing, like ostracised Mary Paynham, that all actions are based on sex. The last part of the book, not included in the truncated and abridged serial version, records Diana's slow movement towards accepting Redworth as her husband. The author must convince the reader that Redworth is a fitting mate for Diana: his sobriety, his 'calculations', his restraint, and Diana's cavalier treatment of him, have all served to diminish him. In the last section of the book his stature is deliberately enlarged. He is shown, not as a speculator in railway shares, but as a countryman. Diana says of him: 'He does not supply me with similes—he points to the source of them'. The 'source of them' is in fact Nature. Diana, who in her convalescence had 'stood out of the sun', is proposed to by Redworth in the glow of sunset. The earlier course of the book emphasised the element of 'worth' in his name: now it is the 'red' of sun and passion which is presented. Although his signification changes, he remains primarily a representative figure, not an individual. Like others of Meredith's late heroes he is too integrated to be interesting.

Diana, having accepted his offer of marriage in a mood of grudging acquiescence ('Banality, thy name is marriage'), imagines them living companionably 'unvexed by that barbarous old fowl and falcon interlude' (xliii; 483). He suddenly embraces her (repeating the act which had twice earlier driven her into panic behaviour, marriage and betrayal): this time 'a big storm-wave caught her from shore and whirled her to mid-sea, out of every sensibility but the swimming one of her loss of self in the man' (xliii; 483). Her brain is 'a fire-fount. This was not like being seated on a throne'. Her soul which had previously hovered on the cliff's edge is now out at sea. She finds herself for the first time freed from her fear of sexual invasion, content to be mastered. Like a good many other novels the book ends with a wedding—but it avoids that complacent patterning which makes all past experience simply a way forward to a satisfactory resting-place. Diana's devious self as well as her generosity persists.

In the last section of the book Meredith achieves remarkable realism in his portrayal of emotion: even the prickly, stilted wit with which Diana receives Redworth's courtship is acutely placed. He no longer feels that pressure to protect his heroine from criticism which had confused the end of the affair with Dacier. In the personality of Diana, Meredith asserts the principle of change—the change of flux rather than of progress. He gives form to this perception in the imagery of Diana, many-aspected moon goddess, as well as in the diverse acts of the woman hounded by 'self'.

In his preceding novel, *The Tragic Comedians*, he had shown the disaster which was brought about by the lovers' insistence on acting out the exalted personality-roles which they had selected for themselves—roles which excluded much that was basic in their natures such as fear and aggression. In *Diana* the heroine has an image of herself which is both refined and self-denigratory. She believes herself to be intellectual and cold, since her intelligence and her independence are the qualities which attract attention and which she can accept without fear. She is forced to recognise that she is also impulsive, hysterical and passionate: it is only when she has accepted the whole range of her personality that she can achieve the warmth of her relationship with Redworth. 'Let me be myself, whatever the martyrdom', she cries early in her ordeal (x; 117). Meredith's perceptions about personality in this novel parallel those of Lawrence about the ego:

> All things flow and change, and even change is not absolute. The whole is a strange assembly of apparently incongruous parts, slipping past one another.
>
> . . . . .
>
> In all this change, I maintain a certain integrity. But woe betide me if I try to put my finger on it. If I say of myself, I am this, I am that!—then, if I stick to it, I turn myself into a stupid fixed thing like a lamp-post.

Diana of the Crossways is essentially an exploratory work: its weaknesses derive from Meredith's uncertainties when glimpsing the implications of what he explores. He distrusts the absolute, hierarchical view of the moral quality of acts but he cannot bring himself entirely to reject it. Therefore he tries to defend Diana conventionally at the same time that he is suggesting that she needs no defence. He bludgeons us into admitting what we need only to perceive. And he becomes so engrossed with the ego of his heroine that he begins to live within it, and fails to animate those about her or to make actual the world beyond her immediate circle.

Technically the book is original in its mingling of realist and symbolist techniques: 'facts' and 'myths' are given equal meaning within the work. It is a profoundly suggestive study of personality in action. In *One of Our Conquerors*, six years later, the contemporary world, interior consciousness, and the symbolic world of music, come together with strange violence in a disturbing exploration of disintegrating identity.

Meredith started more possibilities than he could pursue in his late novels. *One of Our Conquerors*, for all its massive splendours, is at times barely readable because the reader is persistently and deliberately rejected by the florid style. The narration frequently obliterates all traces of ordinary human speech: Nesta smiles 'like the moral crepuscular of a sunlighted day down a not totally inanimate Sunday London street'. *Diana of the Crossways*, though sometimes laborious reading, leaves a vivid and coherent impression because of Meredith's response to his heroine. This response (which rules out objective 'realism') is love. In *The Tragic Comedians* Meredith underwent Alvan's disillusionment with Clotilde, and the various stages of revision show his animus against her increasing. In *Diana* the stages of revision show the contrary process at work. The novel's realism is limited and its generosity of perception enhanced by the author's romance with his heroine.

6

The Amazing Marriage
A Study in Contraries

The Amazing Marriage was the last novel Meredith completed. It was serialised and published in two volumes in 1895 when he was sixty-seven. The novel was not so much the fruit of his old age as an organic growth which had been developing and changing through the previous fifteen years of his life. He began it in 1879 immediately after finishing *The Egoist*, turned to it at intervals, and finally completed and revised it in 1894. It seems that Meredith first conceived it as a relief from the dry light of comedy which plays over *The Egoist*: *The Amazing Marriage* was to satisfy that other half of himself which he had not been able to express through comedy's tart rationality. In *The Amazing Marriage* he combines the generosity of a romantic folk-tale with the acuity of psychological analysis. It is a marriage quite as amazing as that of the principal characters, Carinthia and Lord Fleetwood—and seemingly as unlikely to succeed. The artistic debate between romance and realism is made a part of the book's total meaning; until gradually the reader is led to see that it is not simply *relevant* to the story Meredith is telling but is the same story couched in other terms.

The book is Meredith's attempt to reconcile in an artistic whole the contradictory attractions which had beset him throughout his career: his admiration for simplicity and his talent for representing complexity in human personality; his craftsman's pleasure in dramatic plot structure and his recognition that much significant human emotion has no dynamic pattern; his delight in fantasy and his almost religious feeling for 'reality'. The book is conceived on a heroic scale. The emotional range is unusually wide; in part this is because Meredith withdraws the scrutiny of the Comic Spirit. Both hero and heroine are markedly impervious to ridicule and this allows their battle to be played out on a far wider emotional front than in *The Egoist*. The principal characters in *The Amazing Marriage* are clearly related to character-types who have appeared before in Meredith's work (there are particularly clear parallels with Emilia's simple and passionate nature and Wilfrid Pole's wish to enjoy without debtorship for the thing done in *Sandra Belloni*). But Carinthia and Lord Fleetwood are created on a grander scale and are both endowed with the dangerous nobility of absolute will. They are judged not in relation to 'good citizenship' and society, but in relation to what Meredith sees as the natural laws of our being. In keeping with this, the basic plot has a folk-simplicity: a rich young nobleman asks a mountain-bred girl to marry him on a moment's impulse. He repents his action but goes through with the marriage, abandoning her after one night because his pride is affronted by his situation. Too late, after the birth of the son of his marriage, he comes to realise that he loves her but by that time suffering has killed her love for him. This, at its simplest, is the 'story' of the novel, but Meredith fragments it by the variety of his narrative methods and counterpoints the simple story with an intricate study of 'the reasons and the change of reasons' which express human particularity.

The novel is constructed upon a series of unresolved contraries: the primary one is that between Carinthia's instinctive strength and simplicity, and the tortuous sophistication of Fleetwood's emotions—which take on the guise of a specious rationality, and at times, of an almost equally specious romanticism. Although the opposition between their characters is extreme, it is not simply judged: Carinthia's directness makes her inflexible, her suffering makes her rigorous not generous, and by the end of the book she has stiffened into an emblematic figure remote from the eager girl of the mountain opening. Fleetwood, beset by contradictory impulses (his yearning towards simplicity and his defence of his own complexity), emerges by the end of the book as an intricately recognisable human being instead of a folk villain. At the same time the actual events of the story oblige us to remember that Fleetwood is responsible for his own and Carinthia's suffering. The counterstressing of our sympathies is partly brought about by the different narrative methods which Meredith uses when presenting the hero and heroine.

From the moment when Fleetwood first sees Carinthia, climbing with perfect assurance among the rocks at dawn, she is kept at a distance from the reader and her feelings can only be deduced from the knowledge of her which the first chapters of the book have given. Moreover, we must frequently deduce her feelings against the grain of the events as they appear to some other character. Throughout the central section of the book we are circumscribed by Fleetwood's consciousness and must oppose his dominance in order to reach a just understanding: this has the effect of making the reader occupy a situation analogous to that of Carinthia. Thus, the journey to the prize-fight to which Fleetwood cynically takes Carinthia after their wedding is seen almost entirely through his eyes; ironically, this invests Carinthia's rare remarks with great poignancy. As the book goes on, however, the imaginative leap needed to retain our hold on Carinthia becomes greater. The incidents involving her are invariably presented in retrospect through the accounts of a host of different characters all primarily interested in defending their own area of the action. Occasionally, a vividly idealised picture of Carinthia's behaviour is given by Woodseer, the lover of nature. More often the events are pieced together through rumours, exclamations and denials on the part of other characters.

When Carinthia, estranged from Fleetwood, defends him from a rabble in a London park, the incident is first disclosed through the report of a member of the crowd who knows nothing of what it means, and amplified through the unsympathetic comments of the social women, Livia and Henrietta. The comedy and the grotesquerie of the situation remain: all feeling is removed.

It is as though the reader must undergo Fleetwood's estrangement from her and it is only when he makes his first tentative move towards reconcilement that Carinthia reappears in her own person. However, although we follow the story largely through the mind of Fleetwood, we differ from him in that we know Carinthia. The first section of the book, in which she plays the central role and is presented to us with a happy mingling of robust dialogue and lyrical description, acts as a control on Fleetwood's understanding of events. We are not tempted into his mistake of despising her: rather, the combination of sympathy, bewilderment and respect Carinthia arouses, forces us into something like a myth-making situation in order to combine the disparate emotional elements: Carinthia is gradually transformed from a girl (albeit a 'Beautiful Gorgon—a haggard Venus') into an Amazonian earth-goddess who grows wherever she is planted. With Fleetwood, however, we constantly know as much and more about the intricacies of his feelings as he knows himself, by means of Meredith's use of interior monologue ranging through various levels of consciousness. Fleetwood's characteristic method of controlling the world and shielding himself from self-judgment is that of irony. By presenting his ironic thoughts in an objectified narrative form without commentary from the author Meredith makes it appear that the reader is undertaking an independent act of judgment: the reader's scrutinising awareness outtops Fleetwood's irony and thus 'places' him. In the last part of the book, where Fleetwood is moving painfully towards a discovery of his love, the reader's narrative situation changes.

We are no longer at odds with his interpretation of events (which had earlier preserved us in a role like that of Carinthia); instead, the emotional and grammatical intimacy with which his feelings are rendered has the effect of involving us in them, so that we feel rebuffed with him when Carinthia refuses to be reconciled at the end of the book.

Meredith's narrative techniques grew more varied in his later novels, but he usually retained a controlling narrative *persona* to oversee the action. In *The Amazing Marriage*, however, he constructs his other crucial pair of contraries in the role of the narrator. The controlling narrative is divided between Dame Gossip and a modern analytical novelist of the Meredithian kind—though not wholly to be identified with Meredith. There is thus no final authority to whom we may turn for our reading of events. The reader becomes the arbitrator. Meredith had first used the device of narrative debate in *Sandra Belloni* (1864): in that book the Philosopher is a defensive exaggeration of Meredith's own methods. Meredith pretends impatience with the Philosopher, mocks his insistence on the importance of trivial events and on the analysis of the conflicting motives implicit in an action, and thus ironically asserts his own comparative moderation and commonsense. In *The Amazing Marriage* the device is far more continuously used and is handled with far greater complexity of meaning. The organising fiction of the narrative is that Dame Gossip has handed over the documents of the story to the Novelist but is now much alarmed at the use he is making of them.[1] He is concerned to probe and analyse, confident that human actions are finally explicable if we are prepared to study motives. Dame Gossip, on the contrary, loves the fabulous; to her the story is material for ballads, for homespun moral saws, and for uncritical sympathy. Her view of events synthesises but simplifies.

The debate between Dame Gossip and the Novelist is not merely a technical game. The conflict between their attitudes to action and character (implicit in the different story-telling methods they use) is part of the substance of the novel's meaning, at times running parallel to the conflict between Carinthia's instinctive actions and Fleetwood's complex motives for inaction. In Dame Gossip's telling, the amazing marriage is a folk tale, peopled with characters of absolute virtue and wickedness: the mysteries of human behaviour remain mysteries. It is a flatteringly heroic view of human nature, and Fleetwood at one point adopts it to hide from himself: 'Glimpses of the pictures his deeds painted of him since his first meeting with this woman had to be shunned. He threw them off; they were set down to the mystery men are' (xxviii; 291).

Dame Gossip believes in the fixity of personality (combined with overnight conversions), whereas the Novelist scrutinises the labyrinthine ways through which personality finds issue in action and is modified by completed action. Dame Gossip is a myth-maker; the Novelist (as he claims himself) a historian. Both are indispensable to the novel's full import. This is an attempt to render man's nature in a fully realistic way, recognising the physical basis of our feelings without making physicality the explanation of man; cultivating the 'growing activity of the head' which Meredith saw as the mark of man's continuing evolution; and acknowledging his need for the ideal (or Romance) as well as experience and reflection (Philosophy). The Novelist appeals to posterity, which he claims will 'have studied a developed human nature so far as to know the composition of it a not unequal mixture of the philosophic and the romantic, and that credible realism is to be produced solely by an involvement of those two elements'. Although the Novelist overtly rejects Dame Gossip, the novel itself is implicitly dependent on her for its full effect upon the reader.[2] This is shown structurally: her telling of events opens and ends the book; thus, our expectations are formed by her and we carry her comments away with us.

By using two narrators Meredith is able to vary the tempo

and scale of his narrative. Dame Gossip begins the book with her account of the marriage of Carinthia's parents: the Countess Fanny eloped from her husband when a young woman in her twenties to marry the old Buccaneer, a sailor-hero already in his sixties. The story is presented through ballads and rumours and personal anecdotes from Dame Gossip. A poignant acceptance of the sheer strangeness of human emotions is established in these first three chapters of the book. Meredith uses a heightened vernacular for the Dame which is robust and swift moving but capable of a poetic gravity. The Countess is dying, pining for her son Chillon who is in England and who is incapable of understanding the love which justified his parents' union:

> When there was anything to be done for her, old Kirby was astir. When it was nothing, either in physic or assistance, he was like a great corner of rock. You may indeed imagine grief in the very rock that sees its flower fading to the withered shred. On the last night of her life this old man of past ninety carried her in his arms up a flight of stairs to her bed. (iii; 31)

Meredith uses an even greater range of styles in this book than was usual to him; they are a way of *judging* a scene as well as describing it. The description of Carinthia and Chillon's mountain walk away from their home at the beginning of the main narrative of the book (ch. iv) is grammatically straightforward and vividly pictures the dawnlight:

> Half-way down the ravines it resembled the light cast off a torrent water. It lay on the grass like a sheet of unreflecting steel, and was a face without a smile above. Their childhood ran along the tracks to the forest by the light, which was neither dim nor cold, but grave; presenting tree and shrub and dwarf growth and grass austerely, not deepening or confusing them. (iv; 36)

In contrast, he writes the scene in the gambling casino in an elliptical, tortuously cerebral style which rejects simple statement and uses a hectic plethora of poetical mannerisms. This could be seen simply as Meredith at his worst. In context however, it is clearly a controlled effect, not an assertive self-indulgence on the part of the author.[3] The style suggests the quality of the life described (making the scene an allegory of hell); it also conveys the confused moral response of the young nature-worshipper, Woodseer, through whose eyes it is seen:

> It struck him, that the gamblers had thronged on an invitation to drink the round of seed-time and harvest in a gulp. Again they were desperate gleaners, hopping, skipping, bleeding, amid a whizz of scythe-blades, for small wisps of booty. Nor was it long before the presidency of an ancient hoary Goat-Satan might be perceived, with skew-eyes and pucker-mouth, nursing a hoof on a knee. (ix; 98)

The style Meredith adopts at any moment in the novel is a projection of the consciousness of the person described.

Since however he frequently makes no grammatical or syntactical distinction between the narrator's commentary and the character's thoughts we at first tend to think that we are being presented with an authoritative commentary.

For example, in chapter xvii, 'Records a Shadow Contest Close on the Foregoing': throughout the chapter until the last paragraphs we are within Fleetwood's mind looking out. The speaker shifts from narrator to Fleetwood without notice and the two fuse and separate continuously, the shifts occurring so imperceptibly that we are never certain who is addressing us. The axiomatic statements addressing the reader seem at first to belong to the narrator:

> The madder the world, the madder the fun. And the mixing in it of another element, which it has to beguile us—romance—is not at all bad cookery. Poetic romance is delusion—a tale of a Corsair; a poet's brain, a bottle of gin, and a theatrical wardrobe. Comic romance is about us everywhere, alive for the tapping.
>
> A daughter of the Old Buccaneer should participate in it by right of birth: she would expect it in order to feel herself perfectly at home. Then, be sure, she finds an English tongue and prattles away as merrily as she does when her old scapegrace of a father is the theme. Son-in-law to him! But the path of wisdom runs in the line of facts, and to

have wild fun and romance on this pantomime path, instead of kicking to break away from it, we follow things conceived by the genius of the situation, for the delectation of the fair Countess of Fleetwood and the earl, her delighted husband, quite in the spirit of the Old Buccaneer, father of the bride.

Carinthia sat beside the fire, seeing nothing in the room or on the road. Up in her bedchamber, the girl Madge was at her window. She saw Lord Fleetwood standing alone, laughing, it seemed, at some thought; he threw up his head. Was it a newly married man leaving his bride and laughing? The bride was a dear lady, fit for better than to be driven to look on at a prize-fight—a terrible scene to a lady. She was left solitary: and this her wedding day? The earl had said it, he had said she bore his name, spoke of coming from the altar, and the lady had blushed to hear herself called Miss. The pressure of her hand was warm with Madge: her situation roused the fervent latent sisterhood in the breast of women. (xvii; 180–1)

The savagely gnomic sentences of the first two paragraphs are defined retrospectively as Fleetwood's by the decisive change of style in the third paragraph. The maidservant sees him laughing: he is laughing at the thoughts just recorded. The ensuing sentences mimic Madge's diction and the narrator again disappears, allowing a criticism of Fleetwood's intellectual hysteria to be made by the forthright questions as well as by the girl's response to physical actions: Lord Fleetwood laughing; Carinthia taking her hand. Even the limpidly descriptive sentence 'Carinthia sat beside the fire' does not act solely as narrative. Juxtaposed with Fleetwood's involution and the ironic detachment which makes him speak of himself in the third person, the simplicity of style itself becomes an image of Carinthia.

This quality of impersonation in the narrative complicates even further the question of how far we can rely on the two characterised narrators. The differences between Dame Gossip and the Novelist are not primarily those of style. They are at loggerheads over narrative presentation. The Novelist's case against Dame Gossip is that 'her one idea of animation is to have her *dramatis personae* in violent motion always the biggest foremost'. Although he acknowledges that this makes them credible, he claims: 'The fault of the method is, that they do not instruct; so the breath is out of them before they are put aside'. She does not understand the significance of the actions she describes because she ignores the secondary characters who look on:

> Hence her endless ejaculations over the mystery of Life, the inscrutability of character,—in a plain world, in the midst of such readable people! To preserve Romance (we exchange a sky for a ceiling if we let it go), we must be inside the heads of our people as well as the hearts, more than shaking the kaleidoscope of hurried spectacles, in days of a growing activity of the head. (xx; 209)

Although the Novelist is obviously to a considerable extent Meredith's own spokesman, his explanation does not really tally with the effect of the novel as a whole. He misrepresents the Dame's method, and he himself shows us how impenetrable personality can be. As the book goes on, Dame Gossip's authority grows, so that in a chapter like 'A Survey of the Welsh Cavaliers' (ch. xxxiv) her view of events is no longer challenged by the Novelist. The Novelist has claimed to be a Historian but here he says: 'Poetry, however erratic, is less a servant of the bully Present, or pompous Past, than History. The Muse of History has neither the same divination of the intrinsic nor the devotion to it' (xxxiv; 353).

This is the structural tension which knits together the technical and emotional levels of the book. Dame Gossip's primitive story-telling, which insists on 'pictures' and 'actions', ranges her beside the uncivilised, instinctive personality of Carinthia. The sophisticated complexity of the Novelist's narrative aligns him with Fleetwood. The dispute between the Novelist and Dame Gossip becomes a sort of comic, technical version of the dispute between Fleetwood and Carinthia: he analyses, she synthesises.

Meredith is giving external form to the two major conflicts which dogged him throughout his career as a novelist and attempting to resolve them within an artistic structure. He admired epic actions. Large simple natures existing on a single level of consciousness attracted him emotionally, but whenever he began to scrutinise characters in action he became aware of the intricate mesh of motivation and counter-impulse stemming from various levels of the personality. His novels therefore excel in showing the effects of impulsive acts in which we are momentarily committed to action without implication. His plots are rarely dynamic. He presents action at an extremely slow tempo diffused through the characters' stream of consciousness; or else it happens offstage and is examined only in its effects; sometimes he cuts the knot by 'giving' actions without accounting for them. All these methods are used in *The Amazing Marriage*.

The second conflict, related to this problem of action and consciousness, was that Meredith had two ultimately irreconcilable ideals of the novel: although he devoted much of his career to exploring more and more elaborate ways of rendering human personality in his narrative, he continued to admire the kind of novel which approximates to drama.

The Shaving of Shagpat at the start of his career had shown his feeling for story-telling and his delight in incident. Henry James's affectionately irritated account demonstrates Meredith's faith in plot even late in his career:

> dear great George Meredith once began to express to me what a novel he had just started (One of Our Conquerors) was to be about by no other art that by simply naming to me the half-dozen occurrences, such as they were, that occupied the pages he had already written; so that I remained, I felt, quite without an answer to my respectful enquiry—which he had all the time the very attitude of kindly encouraging and rewarding![4]

The story-telling Dame Gossip, who is treated with facetious scorn by the Novelist, comes to represent for Meredith not only the public demand for 'surface flashes' (ch. xlvi) but the side of his own artistic nature which delighted in the fabulous and wished to express reality through events rather than through analysis. Dame Gossip speaks in the book's last paragraph. (This paragraph is not in the typescript printers' copy at the Pierpont Morgan Library and so is probably a very late addition.) Her language is no longer easily distinguishable from that of Meredith—and her apology placed in so final a position reads like Meredith's own:

> So much I can say: the facts related, with some regretted omissions, by which my story has so skeleton a look, are those that led to the lamentable conclusion. But the melancholy, the pathos of it, the heart of all England stirred by it, have been—and the panting excitement it was to every listener—sacrificed in the vain attempt to render events as consequent to your understanding as a piece of logic, through an exposure of character! Character must ever be a mystery, only to be explained in some degree by conduct; and that is very dependent upon accident: and unless we have a perpetual whipping of the tender part of the reader's mind, interest in invisible persons must needs flag. (xlvii; 510)

As he revised Meredith *removed* motives which he explained in the earlier manuscript versions of the book.[5] This runs counter to his usual method of elaborating as he revises and it shows him moving towards a folk tale presentation of his story—something closer to the manner of Dame Gossip. In both early versions there is a scene after Fleetwood sees Carinthia climbing at dawn. In it, Fleetwood, tormented by his infatuation with Henrietta and jealous of her attachment to Chillon, asks Henrietta to marry him. The scene is long, vividly dramatised, and mainly dialogue. It is with this episode dominant in our minds that we hear of his proposal to Carinthia that night at the ball. Whereas in the final version the proposal is presented as a fact, absolute and full of hope, in the early versions a psychological explanation is provided which removes it from the pristine world of the fairy-tale and sets it immediately in a familiar world of mixed motives and disappointment. This makes it a 'plain world' filled with 'readable people' such as the Novelist demands. But making us superior in knowledge to Carinthia would lessen the absoluteness of her hold upon our imaginations in the first part of the book, which Meredith needs in order to retain our sympathy with her when she is later withdrawn. The motivation of Fleetwood in the early versions, though more easily explicable, is less profound; the proposal derives from momentary pique rather than from some deep but imperfectly acknowledged need in his nature.

In the published version Meredith demonstrates, as in *The Tragic Comedians* and *Diana of the Crossways*, that acts of impulse come not from the surface of personality but from its depths. His revisions of *The Amazing Marriage* move towards accepting the value (even if it be a limited value) of the external, absolute story-telling methods which he associates with the Dame. So, we have additional, secondary evidence that Meredith is not to be identified solely with the Novelist of the book. He realises the division in his own artistic nature in the debate between Dame Gossip and the Novelist.

In this novel Meredith uses a protean artistry to give form to truths which he feels to be absolute: 'Men hating Nature are insane. Women and Nature are close. If it is rather general to hate Nature and maltreat women, we begin to see why the world is a mad world' (xxxv; 363).[6] Through its diversities and contraries the novel expresses the longing for an integrated life. The facetious tone he uses in the debate between Dame Gossip and the Novelist may seem out of key with his complex appraisal of the tragic marriage. In the later part of the novel, certainly, Meredith sometimes uses the Dame's interventions simply to hurry on the narrative. Nevertheless, the jarring discord of the technical dispute becomes part of the larger meaning of the book—the immense difficulties which beset the marriage of instinct and reason. These difficulties are as central to Meredith's art as they are to the relationships of his people.

The technical dispute acts out the sheer irritation which is a large part of a failing relationship. This allows a full, humane and uninhibited seriousness to his study of the marriage itself. In *The Amazing Marriage* Meredith shows a tenderness to his characters which ranges far beyond the rational appraisal of comedy towards acceptance of the strangeness of human emotion: a strangeness which can be scrutinised but not explained away.

Conclusion

MEREDITH never thoroughly trusted his readers. Despite the growing critical enthusiasm for his work his sense of being at odds with the reading public intensified in the later years of his career. 'Readers of Novels read not for the sake of judging human nature but to escape from it', he observed in an unpublished note dating from the eighteen-eighties. Writing to George Stevenson in January 1888 just as he was beginning *One of Our Conquerors* he mentions the rising American sales of his books and comments: 'I am . . . disdainful of an English public, and am beset by the devils of satire when I look on it. That is not a good state for composition.' (*Letters*, ii, 406) Victor Radnor in *One of Our Conquerors* summarises the English view of the novel, as Meredith interpreted it: 'If I read fiction, let it be fiction; airier than hard fact . . . I can't read dull analytical stuff or "stylists" when I want action—if I'm to give my mind to a story. I can supply the reflections' (xviii; 194). Victor is a particularly unreflective man.

There are a number of reasons for Meredith's radical, and perhaps exaggerated, mistrust of the reading public. His forty years as publisher's reader for Chapman and Hall meant that he had to spend a good deal of his time reading manuscripts by writers with 'ability below the level of a commonplace theme'. Though he was occasionally able to encourage high talent, such as that of Hardy and Gissing, most of the time he was reading great numbers of inferior manuscripts, feebly treating well-worn themes of the day. His preference as reader is for books on birds, and anthropological subjects. In his comments on novels he emphasises conventional requirements such as the importance of plot, of 'good style', of characters who 'hold attention'. His job is primarily to decide what the public will like. He sometimes rejects interesting work because the story is 'repulsive' or 'disagreeable' or 'afflicting'. The acid summaries show what Meredith expected of a novelist who hoped to sell his work:

In low relief by Morley Roberts.

An artist and a sort of journalist fall in love with a girl, who is a 'model', and is beautiful and pure. They converse in couples. They do nothing else. She in the end likes one better than the other. That is all. There is no story. The conversations are fairly natural; not strong enough to support a volume. Here are two.

He complains frequently of 'sawdust dialogue'; 'over-accentuating, explaining too much'; 'The scenes are narrated, as by a cleverish clerk on the spot, but they are not presented'; 'the author's purpose is the one thing manifest'; 'too much empty dialogue and no story'; 'the writer has not imagination to present pictures of adventures'; 'plodding style'; and 'Page upon page of roundabout, in attempted expression of the commonest things—like a scrupulous village wife's yarn'.

Some of these comments, particularly the last, remind one of critics' objections to Meredith's own work; it is revealing to observe how much more orthodox than his own practice are his demands as publisher's reader where he is also judging what will be acceptable.

Many of the novels, even if rejected by Chapman and Hall—as *East Lynne* was on Meredith's advice—were published elsewhere with considerable success. The disparity between such work and his own must have intensified his sense of isolation and his defensive disdain for the reading public. Being an artist of integrity as well as high vanity he determined to distinguish himself by every stylistic means from the herd of lesser writers and to turn his back on the popularity which came easily to them.

The attacks on the 'low ethical tone' of *Richard Feverel* and *Modern Love* at the beginning of his career, and Mudie's refusal to circulate the novel, also had repercussions for many years in Meredith's art. It was not until the eighteen-eighties that he turned anew to the theme of marriage; by then he had created a subtle network of sexual metaphor which went beyond the double-entendre of which Hardman complained in *Sandra Belloni*.

His sense of isolation never left him and he attributed it to the neglect he had suffered in the earlier part of his career. In the late Black Notebook he wrote: 'I courted none—therefore I rep[ined] in poverty and obscurity; and those [who] do so, have in their veins a sourne[ss] that no plenitude of subseque[nt] Autumnal sunsfire can sweeten.' His period of 'Autumnal sunsfire' was clouded by his wife's death and his own increasing deafness and ataraxy—all of which forced further isolation upon him. In another unpublished note pencilled in his late uncontrolled script—a script which is the wreck of his earlier exquisite and fastidious hand—he observed: 'The state of ataraxy is the threshold of Nirvana; & it is found to be so complete in itself that those who have entered in it cherish no wish to step beyond. Only those who have not attained to it desire Nirvana.'

The last years of his creative life thrust him beyond his earlier delight in consciousness and conversation. Writing to Morley some time after his wife's death he said: 'The thought often uppermost is in amazement at the importance we attach to our hold of sensation. So much grander, vaster, seems her realm of silence' (*Letters*, ii, 377). In *One of Our Conquerors*, which he wrote at this period, he tested the area of his artistry to its limits, moving beyond comedy, articulateness, even at times beyond metaphor in his attempt to register those levels of the inner life where language can get no purchase.[2] It is, self-consciously, a novel about language and the limits of language. At times it inadvertently oversteps those limits. At other times, it deliberately explores the territory beyond them. Morally, the novel examines the responsibilities which are imposed by consciousness and articulation. Decoratively, it allows Meredith to try out linguistic effects which repudiate the reader.

In *One of Our Conquerors*, perhaps for the first time, Meredith seems to have despaired of language as true communication. Victor likes phrases because they 'raise and limit' experience. Nataly, his devoted common-law wife, is reflective by temperament but withheld by fear from formulation: what is formulated cannot be ignored. Nesta, their intelligent daughter, shows the potentialities of unanalysed responsiveness. In another late note Meredith remarked: 'There is deeper than what a man speaks, though sometimes the bubble comes from the depths.' All the significant scenes between the characters in this novel take place in silence. Colney Durance's serial story 'The Rival Tongues' represents the babel of languages playing on the surface of experience.

Music becomes here the liberating alternative to speech. The conquerors in the novel are Victor Radnor, Wagner and death. Music was necessary to the world of Meredith's novels from the start of his career. He knew that his struggle with language must of its very nature leave him worsted. The 'high notes and condensings' of his comedies perfectly render the point where consciousness comes into focus; but throughout his life he was also concerned with 'the submerged self—self in the depths'. As early in his career as *Sandra Belloni* Meredith seems to have sensed that opera, in particular, could achieve something he was seeking in his novels: a marriage between epic action and the subtle articulation of feeling. In opera the surge of events is suspended and resolved at intervals in the intense expressiveness of aria. Meredith responded to opera's stylisation of experience: the way in which its pace is controlled by emotion rather than the exigencies of the 'box-like' plot. Moreover music freed him from the stress of language: it suggested the numinous. It is untranslatable. Characters in the novels are frequently judged not only by their responsiveness to music but also by their taste in composers: Rosamund is surprised by Dr Shrapnel's love of a Mozart requiem; Diana listens to Chopin; Victor Radnor enjoys Donizetti but is overpowered, unwillingly, by Wagner. In *One of Our Conquerors* music is not simply a literary symbol; it is essential to the experience which the novel expresses. Meredith gives us precise references and expects us to hear the music within ourselves, supplementing the words on the page.

In *One of Our Conquerors* Meredith, fanatical believer in words, attempts to reach the territory of the unconscious, of madness and of death, where words give place to sound and effects of motion. Or to silence. It is a strange, compelling, hideously difficult experiment. It is the cryptic expression of his sense of alienation from the reader and of the disruption between man's social self and his deepest personality processes. Within the artistry of the novel music becomes a moving though partial solution to his intractable dilemma over language.

'I myself am as a describer of nature and natural emotions', Meredith wrote to his son Arthur in 1881, 'a constant sufferer in dealing with a language part of which is dead matter' (*Letters*, i, 321). He sometimes rationalised this attribute of language into a division between the 'Celtic' and 'Teutonic' elements in English; in his novels he struggled to avoid the merely familiar. He attempted to build up language from perceptions afresh and oblige the reader to act out for himself the thing described rather than accept it as something foreknown. The narrative rhetoric of the books does not suggest the speaking voice—the sound of conversation or monologue—as in Dickens's novels, where repetition, exclamation and a syntactical piling of phrase on phrase reach their full expressiveness only when read aloud. Meredith's work, by contrast, supposes a silent reader, the sentence structures moving in the mind and becoming assimilated to one's own processes of consciousness. Contrasted rhythmical movements convey the characters' feelings and modes of thought as surely as do imagery and analysis. Grammar and syntax have a heightened role, constantly shifting us in and out of twisting consciousnesses and epigrammatic formulations. 'One cannot pursue to conclusions a line of meditation that is half-built on the sensations as well as the mind', comments the narrator in *Beauchamp's Career*.

Meredith mistrusted his reader partly because he gave him so vital a part to play in the re-creation of the novel's experience. Sometimes the quiddities of his writing become mere ornamentation and the thronging pages submerge the sustained narrative meaning, offering, as Henry James commented of *Lord Ormont and His Aminta*, 'All the elaborate predicates of exposition without the ghost of a nominative to hook themselves to'.[3] Meredith makes at times almost unconscionable demands on our activity as readers (as in his disordering of chronology and suppression of connections). *The Pall Mall Gazette* in its notice of *Rhoda Fleming* (26 October 1865) neatly characterises one method by which Meredith avoids conventional 'plot':

> Instead of unfolding his drama before our eyes, instead of letting the reader see the evolution of events, he presents a succession of scenes in which people are engaged in matters and conversation often wholly irrelevant to the action of his story, and they casually let fall remarks which inform us of this or that important event having taken place.

Forster's description of 'Meredithian plot' as 'resembling a series of kiosks most artfully placed among the wooded slopes, which his people reach by their own impetus, and from which they emerge with altered aspect' hints at this same secrecy.[4] Meredith turns away from conventional plot so far that he rarely shows us the momentary crisis of external action. Yet it is also true that his novels in memory resolve themselves into remarkably vivid 'scenes'. The same thing happens with the novels of Samuel Richardson and Virginia Woolf. This is surely because the method of these three closely-related writers is to engage us in the flux of experience in a manner parallel to the processes of life.

Being without an independent income Meredith found himself constantly driven towards 'a spanking bid for popularity' and yet always unable to conform to the demands for dynamic plot and climax: 'I do not make a plot', he wrote to Bainton in 1887. 'If my characters, as I have them at heart, were boxed in a plot, they would soon lose the lines of their features.' And in old age he told Clodd: 'I never outline my novels before starting on them; I live night and day with my characters.'[5] And to Baker he claimed: 'But I have never started on a novel to pursue the theory it developed. The dominant idea in my mind took up the characters and the story midway' (*Letters*, ii, 398).

All these comments date from the last phase of his career; they sound a long way from his comment in the *Westminster Review* in 1857: 'After a satisfactory construction of plot, when to dramatise and when to narrate, is the novelist's lesson.'[6] Yet Meredith was learning 'the novelist's lesson' throughout his creative life. His repudiation of box-like plot meant that he was obliged to find alternative ordering processes for his novels. He shaped his books primarily by varying the tempo at which action is recorded. Events rarely reach us intact; they come refracted through the wishes and dreads of the characters. He fused the narrator's commentary with the character's stream-of-consciousness; this creates a fluid form for our experience as readers but it does not absolve us from the need to judge. Indeed the most arresting of his organising techniques is his way of forcing on the reader a variety of conflicting roles within the novel. In some ways the organisation of Meredith's novels *depends* upon conflict between author and reader. Moreover Meredith seems to have needed to sense a hostile public in order to give form (and limits) to his experiments. The vivid achievement of the novels is inhibited by Meredith's uneasiness about the implications of his perceptions.

The range and power of his novels, their interpenetration of lyricism and comedy, their fierce mining for the sources of human personality, their richness of invention and perception, tempt me to praise them even beyond their achievement. Historically, they are close to the source of much that has been most fruitful in the twentieth-century novel in English. But they are limited by a final timidity in Meredith's artistic personality: a refusal to be committed to his perceptions, a tendency to grimace belligerently at his reader. He mocked this trait with typically involuted awareness in the satirical observer-author Colney Durance, whose 'pretentious and laboured' satiric epic in *One of Our Conquerors* forms a weak shadow to the book's theme:

> 'He is unsuccessful and embittered', said Victor to Nesta. 'Colney will find in the end, that he has lost his game and soured himself by never making concessions. Here's this absurd Serial—it fails, of course; and then he has to say, it's because he won't tickle his English, won't enter into a "frowzy complicity" with their tastes'. (xxxvi; 434)

Even in this passage it is hard to tell whether Victor or Durance or Meredith is being most mocked.

Meredith may sometimes have exaggerated the isolation in which he was carrying out his experiments with the novel. By the eighteen-eighties Henry James was alongside him. George Eliot attained something of the same mandarin complexity in the eighteen-seventies with *Daniel Deronda*. His relinquishing of the idea that a novel should be universally readable did mean, however, that he was able to experiment far more radically than his contemporaries with the language of the novel and with the *flux*, as distinct from the *development*, of character.

In *Richard Feverel* he looked to a psychologically acute future audience 'to whom it will be given to see the elementary machinery at work; who, as it were, from some slight hint of the straws, will feel the winds of March when they do not blow' (xxv; 233). He was well aware of the dangers of innovation. In the Blue Notebook there is a portentous observation dating from the early eighteen-sixties: 'If an innovator be not a giant, he does for himself a foolish business, & for the world something next to useless. Let him rest and philosophise. His task is to enjoy what he knows, & to conform.'

But Meredith himself never was content to conform. He always balances on the edge of rejection. He inverts, re-interprets, explores, the norms of the novel form and of his own society. The struggle to fuse the actual and the ideal, to describe accurately without reducing the penumbra of possibilities, preoccupied him throughout his creative life. The image of the novelist as anatomist or miner, and the image of the two false colourings—rose pink and dirty drab—recur insistently.[7] In one of his earlier, most complete statements outside the novels he wrote to Jessopp (20 September 1864):

Between realism and idealism there is no natural conflict. This completes that. Realism is the basis of good composition: it implies study, observation, artistic power, and (in those who can do no more) humility. Little writers should be realistic. They would then at least do solid work. They afflict the world because they will attempt that it is given to none but noble workmen to achieve. A great genius must necessarily employ ideal means, for a vast conception cannot be placed bodily before the eye, and remains to be suggested. Idealism is as an atmosphere whose effects of grandeur are wrought out through a series of illusions, that are illusions to the sense within us only when divorced from the ground-work of the real. Need there be exclusion, the one of the other? The artist is incomplete who does this. Men to whom I bow my head (Shakespeare, Goethe; and in their way, Molière, Cervantes) are Realists au fond. But they have the broad arms of Idealism at command. They give us Earth; but it is earth with an atmosphere. One may find as much amusement in a Kaleidoscope as in a merely idealistic writer: and just as sound prose is of more worth than pretentious poetry, I hold the man who gives a plain wall of fact higher in esteem than one who is constantly shuffling the clouds and dealing with airy, delicate sentimentalities, headless and tailless imaginings, despising our good plain strength (*Letters*, i, 156)

Meredith's defence of the marriage of realism and idealism persists, but his championship of one or the other varies at different periods of his career. In the eighteen-fifties and sixties writers such as Stendhal and Flaubert were little appreciated in England and the tendency was (as in Ruskin) to insist on observation finally as a way of interpreting the parable of the universe rather than for its own sake. At that time Meredith emphasised the importance of scrutinising our emotions, of avoiding the transcendental, of recognising the devious and the complicated. *Richard Feverel* and *Sandra Belloni* are in their different ways both attacks on sentimental idealism. In the eighteen-seventies when Meredith was much involved with the *Fortnightly*, its editor Morley, and liberal thinking generally, he again reacted against his environment and scrutinised the rationalism by which he was surrounded, emphasising the unaccommodated role of fantasy in our lives (*The Adventures of Harry Richmond*) or the temperamental sources of political thought (*Beauchamp's Career*). In the eighteen-eighties and nineties when fashion favoured French writers such as Mendès who 'monsterised' Zola with their 'cataturient' realism, he moved to defend the sense of the ideal within us, couching it in terms of aspiration, albeit thwarted, or romance. *Lord Ormont and His Aminta*, one of the few novels with a 'happy' ending shows the unmarried lovers Weyburn and Aminta escaping from her husband Lord Ormont and running a progressive school in Switzerland. This socially conscious conclusion is possible only because of the erotic scene in which Weyburn and Aminta first discover and express their love through swimming together out at sea. The novel is one of Meredith's most forthright though least profound attempts to combine the ideal and the real in the form of freedom and duty.

Meredith's effect on the writers of his own time and the generation which followed establishes him as an artist who 'strikes his impress right and left around him'. Gissing and Hardy both acknowledged the practical encouragement that Meredith had given them early in their careers. Robert Louis Stevenson considered him 'out and away the greatest force in English letters'. Gissing held that 'for the last thirty years he has been producing work unspeakably above the best of any living writer' and Hardy wrote of him:

> He was of those whose wits can shake
> And riddle to the very core
> The counterfeits that Time will break.

All these writers felt the equivocality of his achievement but they united in praising the new freedom and intensity he had brought into the English novel.

Oscar Wilde's 'Vivian' in 'The Decay of Lying' exquisitely formulates the exasperation which at times besets the reader, even one like Vivian who sets Meredith aloft with Balzac:

> Ah! Meredith! Who can define him? His style is chaos illumined by flashes of lightning. As a writer he has mastered everything except language: as a novelist he can do everything except tell a story: as an artist he is everything except articulate. Somebody in Shakespeare—Touchstone, I think—talks about a man who is always breaking his shins over his own wit, and it seems to me that this might serve as the basis for a criticism of Meredith's method.

But as Wilde (or 'Gilbert') says of Meredith in 'The Critic as Artist', 'It is difficult not to be unjust to what one loves'. And in 'The Soul of Man under Socialism' he offered a more wholehearted tribute:

> One incomparable novelist we have now in England, Mr George Meredith. There are better artists in France, but France has no one whose view of life is so large, so varied, so imaginatively true. There are tellers of stories in Russia who have a more vivid sense of what pain in fiction may be. But to him belongs philosophy in fiction. His

people not merely live, but they live in thought. One can see them from myriad points of view. They are suggestive. There is soul in them and around them. They are interpretative and symbolic.

Such praise brings home the extent to which Meredith was 'The Hero as Man-of-Letters' to his fellow authors in the later part of his life. But even more suggestive is the way in which he represents for the next generation of writers the dominating creative presence whom they must escape but can never entirely leave behind. Lawrence wrote deprecatingly that he hoped *The Rainbow* would appeal to the 'Meredithy public'. Forster in *A Room with a View* makes Cyril, damagingly, an admirer of Meredith but the lyricism of the scene of Lucy in the bed of violets calls on the ecstatic language of the scene by the weir with Lucy and Richard in *Richard Feverel.*

The responses of Wilde, of James, of Lawrence, of Forster and of Virginia Woolf all betray admiration and a sense of creative kinship. The range of Meredith's energy is indicated by the protean forms this kinship takes: for Wilde, his epigrammatic formulations and rejection of 'realism'; for James, a late style which abandoned the notion of universal readability and forced the reader to respond at his highest pitch of sensibility; for Lawrence, symbolic organisation of plot and an acknowledgment of woman's sexuality and her search for freedom; for Forster, buoyant heroines, musical imagery, the manipulation of fantasy, and for Virginia Woolf, a rendering of the inner life through moments and symbols rather than plot.

But Meredith's closest kinship is with James Joyce. It is not merely that *The Ordeal of Richard Feverel* had an acknowledged influence on Joyce's early work, or that Meredith's lyricism is consciously imitated in the effulgent description of the girl by the Liffey in *Portrait of the Artist as a Young Man*. In *Ulysses*, among several other allusions, Joyce converts Meredith's most quintessential epigram into a telegraphic admonition which is to reverberate through the novel. The manner of the introduction, moreover, jocund and equivocal, further plays with and illustrates Joyce's feeling of comradeship for his closest predecessor in experimental fiction:

> Do you think it is only a paradox, the quaker librarian was asking. The mocker is never taken seriously when he is most serious.
>
> They talked seriously of mocker's seriousness.
>
> Buck Mulligan's again heavy face eyed Stephen awhile. Then, his head wagging, he came near, drew a folded telegram from his pocket. His mobile lips read, smiling with new delight.
>
> —Telegram! he said. Wonderful inspiration! Telegram! A papal bull!
>
> He sat on a corner of the unlit desk, reading aloud joyfully:
>
> —*The sentimentalist is he who would enjoy without incurring the immense debtorship for a thing done* Signed: Dedalus.[8]

Meredith like Joyce delighted in brilliance and expected his readers to share his delight. If at times the prodigal energy with which he strives to be memorable produces simply an effect of strain, at other times a single image or the whole retrospect of a scene can open up for us new areas of imaginative comprehension. He works not by accretion but by variety. The total effect is of unrest, excitement, growth. Meredith demands of the reader a pitch of receptiveness and of participation more commonly granted to poetry than to the novel. He rewards him with an experience complex, peculiar and vivid.

APPENDIX

Meredith's Notebooks

THE Altschul collection, Yale University Library, includes eight notebooks covering the whole period of Meredith's creative life, as well as two portfolios containing individual pages of notes.

I refer throughout this book to the notebooks by a description of their covers. A strict chronological numbering is not possible since more than one were in use at the same time. Meredith rarely used all the pages in a book. The pages are small (Maroon Notebook, 4 ins × 2½ ins; Blue Notebook, 4½ ins × 3 ins).

1. Maroon Notebook, 104 pp., c. 1857–62. Material used in poems and in *Richard Feverel*, 'Modern Love', *Sandra Belloni*, *Vittoria*; also contains epigrams not used until *Beauchamp's Career* (1876 for 1875), and *Diana of the Crossways* (1885). The notebook from which Meredith read to Hardman on 24 May 1862 (quoted, S. M. Ellis, *George Meredith*, London, 1919, p. 126).

2. Blue Notebook, 112 pp. (3 missing), c. 1858–63. Material used in poems, *Richard Feverel* and *Vittoria*. Topics of 'Pall Mall' articles in front pocket. The notebook used by Meredith while walking in Europe in 1863 (*Letters*, i, 121).

3. Rustic Scene Notebook, 24 pp., c. ?1857–60. The notebook itself contains a sentimental poem in a hand other than Meredith's, and nineteen humorous sketches of smug-looking men. *Inlaid* are four sheets of blue paper, folded, covered in Meredith's exquisite and minute early hand. These sheets contain material used in *Richard Feverel*, *Evan Harrington*, *The Egoist* and *Diana of the Crossways*.

4. Water patterned Notebook, 68 pp., c. ?1860–. Four pages used. Anecdotes, one of them similar to an incident in *Evan Harrington*.

5. Olive Green Notebook (bound in cloth cover with 'Poems' in gold leaf on spine), 56 pp., c. 1873–4. Connected with *Beauchamp's Career*. A collection of anecdotes illustrating different kinds of heroism, military and domestic. Three of the anecdotes concern Admiral (or Colonel) Michell, mentioned in *Beauchamp's Career*, ch. iv; pp. 42, 44 and ch. xi; p. 94 as 'young Michell of the Rodney'.

6. 'Modern Manicheism and Other Poems' in gold on spine, 96 pp., ?1870s. Four anecdotes concerning disastrous marriages—none traced in the novels.

7. Purple silk Notebook, 72 pp., ?1880s. Epigrams and descriptions of Switzerland. No references traced in novels.

8. Black Notebook, 48 pp., c. 1880–93. Material used in *One of Our Conquerors* and *Lord Ormont and his Aminta*: includes a number of comments germane to his inner life. Handwriting at first controlled but last entries in extremely feeble hand. A battered notebook which Meredith seems to have used over a long period from the 1870s into extreme old age.

Portfolios 'Notes on Aristophanes' etc; 'Manuscript of a Dramatic Dialogue' etc. The portfolios contain loose sheets, mostly in random order; some of these sheets are covered in handwriting from more than one period of Meredith's life. They contain stories used in poems, fragments, epigrams, sketches for unwritten novels; the outline of 'Contrivance Jack' and notes on Aristophanes made at the time Meredith was working on the Essay on Comedy.

Meredith's private working notebooks are an extraordinary revelation of his ultimate reserve even with himself. They consist mainly of epigrams, Hardy-esque incidents, anecdotes and description of scenes. The observations most germane to his own life are couched in general terms, while the descriptions of the natural world are the most directly 'personal' entries—the drafts and fragments of poems flow out of these descriptions of the natural world. Their strange relationship to his creative work is expressive of Meredith's peculiar artistic tensions.

Professor Phyllis Bartlett has shown that certain early manuscript poems in the Berg Collection, New York Public Library, which are clearly addressed to his wife, and expressive of lyrical enthusiasm, are used ironically in *Richard Feverel*, where they are assigned to Diaper Sandoe, the poetaster betrayer of Sir Austin, and are admired by the youthful and inexperienced Richard. (Sir Austin's determination to wipe out the poet in Richard by forcing him to burn his own efforts is presented as the crucial moment which begins their irreversible alienation.)

Similarly certain of the observations in the notebooks seem to throw light upon Meredith's own particular experience though they are always couched in general terms: 'In youth we exaggerate our impressions—we force our imaginations voluptuously—hence much of our subsequent disenchantment' (Maroon Notebook) c. 1858; 'Intense love is a violation of life' (Blue Notebook) c. 1860; 'At the period when nature is strongest in us we are the least natural. The reason is simply, that in growing old we can no longer take the trouble to assume a character' (Maroon Notebook) c. 1858. These mordant sayings seem to stem from Meredith's own personal disenchantment of that period—the 'we' of their form is a generalisation which makes it possible for him to recognise his own predicament: 'We can trace our misfortunes to one weakness: but we cannot see that the previous course of our life produced it.'

Only occasionally does he use the form 'I' (a matter of three or four times in eight notebooks), and only once, in the passage I have already quoted in the Conclusion, does he give vent to that chagrin which occurs in his reported speech in old age: 'I courted none—therefore I rep[ined] in poverty and obscurity; and those [who] do so, have in their veins a sourne[ss] that no plenitude of subseque[nt] Autumnal sunsfire can sweeten' (Black Notebook).

This complaint voices an embitterment which parched his spirits and drove him at times to highpitched impeachments of his readers' intelligence.

The notebooks make it clear that Meredith's ideas for his novels germinated over a long period. Remarks and thoughts jotted down will frequently emerge in works written twenty years later. Moreover the lists in the Portfolios suggest that his last five novels (written in the 1880s and 90s) were already in his mind by the early 1870s.

BIBLIOGRAPHICAL NOTE

THE Memorial Edition (27 volumes, London, 1909–11, New York, 1909–12) is the most complete edition of Meredith's prose works. It includes Miscellaneous Prose (vol. 23) and a Bibliography by A. Esdaile and variant readings (vol. 27). The variant readings are not complete. The Standard Edition (15 volumes, 1914–20) follows the same pagination as the Memorial Edition.

At the time I write, *The Poetical Works*, ed. G. M. Trevelyan, 1912, is still the only full edition of the poems, but Professor Phyllis Bartlett's forthcoming edition will shortly supersede it. Similarly, I had access while writing this study only to the volumes of *Letters*, collected and edited by Meredith's son (W. M. Meredith), 2 volumes, 1912, supplemented by other letters published by Bertha Coolidge, R. E. G. George, Arthur Symons and J. O. Baylen. Professor C. L. Cline's new three-volume collection of Meredith's Letters has now become available.

For bibliographies of Meredith's prose and verse and critical studies of his work in the earlier part of this century I would refer the reader to M. Buxton Forman's two books: *A Bibliography of the Writings in Prose and Verse of Meredith*, 1922, and *Meredithiana*, 1924. For a more complete bibliography of Meredith's publications and a list of critical studies and articles up to 1966 the reader can consult the section on Meredith which I have contributed to the *New Cambridge Bibliography of English Literature*, Volume 4. In the course of writing the present study I have read almost everything listed there and my range of debts is wide. I hope

I have acknowledged all direct debts in the notes to this volume.

The manuscript material used in this study is as follows:

Altschul Collection, Yale University Library

Holograph of *The Adventures of Harry Richmond* (complete)
Holograph of *The Tragic Comedians* (complete)
Holograph of *Diana of the Crossways* (fragmentary earlier version)
Holograph of 'A Conqueror in Our Time' (incomplete earlier version of *One of Our Conquerors*)
Holograph of *The Amazing Marriage* (two fragmentary earlier versions)
Holograph of an unpublished incomplete play 'The Satirist'
Meredith's unpublished working notebooks (see Appendix)
Two Portfolios of MS notes headed:
Original MS notes on Aristophanes etc.
Original MS notes for a dramatic dialogue etc.
Meredith's comments as publisher's reader.

Pierpont Morgan Library, New York

Holograph of *Diana of the Crossways* (complete)
Typescript of *The Amazing Marriage* (complete)
Widener Collection, Widener Library, Harvard
Holograph of *The Tale of Chloe* (complete)

NOTES

INTRODUCTION

1 *Sowing* (London, 1960), p. 166. To G. M. Trevelyan and his contemporaries Meredith seemed to rival Tolstoy in creative moral vision while Arthur Symons claimed him as a Decadent: 'Meredith is, in the true, wide sense, as no other English writer of the present can be said to be, a Decadent. What Decadence, in literature, really means is that learned corruption of language by which style ceases to be organic, and becomes, in the pursuit of some new expressiveness of beauty, deliberately abnormal. Meredith's style, unlike many self-conscious styles, is alive in every fibre'. A. Symons, 'George Meredith: with some unpublished letters', *Fortnightly Review*, n.s. cxiii (1923), 62 (quoting his own article first published anonymously in 1898). One of the most trenchant of the contemporary attacks, at a time when Meredith had at last become fashionable, was that of William Watson in 'Fiction—Plethoric and Anaemic', *National Review*, xiv (1889), 167–83. Meredith is the plethoric, James and Howells the anaemic. A veiled apologia for his own style is presented in Meredith's sympathetic analysis of Diana's 'desire to prune, compress, over-charge' and his admission that she 'occasionally preferred commonplaces in gilt, as she was much excited to do' (i; 11–12).

2 Meredith's phrase for the subconscious: 'the submerged self—self in the depths—', *Sandra Belloni*, ch. xxxviii.

3 *The Letters of Henry James*, ed. P. Lubbock (London, 1920), 263.

4 (London, 1934), p. 232. Meredith objected, naturally enough, to criticism which saw his niceties of language as frivolity: 'I am termed a harlequin, a performer of antics. I choose, when I write, the expression seeming to my imagination just, and as it is not conventional, they denounce it. When there is stress of emotion, my speech is necessarily simple, in harmony with the common human element. They admit it, yet cannot allow that at other seasons the writer's fancy (if he have any) should be allowed play'. R. E. G. George, 'Unpublished Letters of George Meredith', *Nineteenth Century*, ciii (1928), 159. The letter is dated 28 June 1887.

5 *Westminster Review*, n.s. xiii (1858).

6 My thanks are due particularly to the Curators of Yale University Library for permission to use Meredith's early or final drafts of *The Adventures of Harry Richmond*, *The Tragic Comedians*, *Diana of the Crossways*, *One of Our Conquerors* and *The Amazing Marriage*, and to the Pierpont Morgan Library for permission to use Meredith's final drafts of *Diana of the Crossways* and *The Amazing Marriage*. See Appendix for an account of Meredith's

Notebooks and Portfolio Notes in the Altschul Collection, Yale University Library.

7 *Victorian Fiction: A Guide to Research*, ed. L. Stevenson (Cambridge, Mass.), 1964.

(1) THE ORDEAL OF RICHARD FEVEREL

1 *Leader*, 5 January 1856. She wrote another review in the *Westminster Review*, n.s. ix (1856), 638: 'it is less an imitation of the "Arabian Nights" than a similar creation inspired by a thorough and admiring study.'

2 See Ch. II, pp. 46–7, and note 12 for a description of 'The Knight-errant of the Nineteenth Century'. Viscountess Milner's account of the plot as projected in 1904 begins: 'A man immensely rich, imbued with Herbert Spencer's ideas, full of the all-importance of the future and its problems, always dwelling in them, always working at them . . . He has a scheme, worked out in conjunction with men of science and enthusiasts, for moving the Earth.' Fragments, such as this from the Portfolio notes, are typical of Meredith's vein of boisterous allegory more akin to *conte* than to novel: 'One who did a great cleansing public service: "For awhile, & for long, after the First of heroes had performed his main & most unsavoury task there clung to him such pervasions of the Augean reek as knocked down men more emphatically than the trained fist of their champion; ladies, on a visit of admiration, fell swooning within a league; kings of the countries he traversed, despatched messengers entreating him to hurry onward his feet; & it was with a roar of melancholy laughter that this glory & pest of men betook himself to his repeated plunge-bath, & submitted to the pouring on of ointments, unguents, essences, fine scents, hateful to his manly nostrils; nor less indeed to his common sense, which well knew how surely it will be when we set a perfume in contention with a stench, that the two, instead of extinguishing either the other, embrace, to create the anti-natural neutral malodour known as the atmosphere of Society. Nevertheless, for the sake of living among his fellows, also, one surmises, in compassion for his legitimate wife, who tottered in his presence, he went through the processes of purification."'

3 *Westminster Review*, n.s. xxvi (1864), 30. See, for example, W. R. Mueller, 'Theological Dualism and the "system" in *Richard Feverel*', *ELH*, xviii (1951); W. H. Marshall, 'Richard Feverel, the Original Man', *Victorian Newsletter*, no. xviii (1960); I. H. Buchen, '*The Ordeal of Richard Feverel*: science versus nature', *ELH*, xxix (1962); J. W. Morris, 'Inherent Principles of Order in *Richard Feverel*', *PMLA*, lxxviii (1963).

4 *Diana of the Crossways*, i; 18. The word 'instructively' is a late insertion by Meredith in the copy to be sent to the printers (Pierpont Morgan Library, MS 35).

5 'Two natures warred in his bosom, or it may have been the Magian conflict still going on' (xliv; 550).

6 F. D. Curtin's article is in *Nineteenth-Century Fiction*, vii (1953).

7 See note 3 above.

8 Quoted S. M. Ellis, *George Meredith* (London, 1919), p. 126. In old age Meredith told Viscountess Milner that 'he had written all the aphorisms in *Richard Feverel* straight off. "I am not responsible for them, they are Sir Austin Feverel's—only one came to me."' 'Talks with George Meredith', *National Review*, cxxxi (1948), 455. The aphorisms used in *Richard Feverel* appear in sequence in the Maroon Notebook; they are all lightly crossed through (Meredith's way of indicating that material has been used)—except one: 'It is frequent to accuse our friends of our own infirmities.' His account of their manner of composition is exactly endorsed.

9 *The Common Reader*, second series (London, 1932), p. 228.

10 *Bibliography and Various Readings*, Memorial Edition (London, 1911), xxvii, 23.

11 Adrian and Mrs Berry—like many of Meredith's most narrowly and symbolically controlled creations—had models in life: Adrian Harley was based on Maurice Fitzgerald, nephew of Edward Fitzgerald, and Mrs Berry on the Merediths' Seaford landlady, Mrs Ockenden. His appropriation of his acquaintances shows the same tart paradoxical process as his use of his own experience and of literary models.

12 Bertha Coolidge, *A Catalogue of the Altschul Collection* (New Haven, 1931), p. 79. Hereafter referred to as Coolidge.

13 Mrs Pauline Simons in an unpublished M.A. thesis for Manchester University elaborates the correspondences between the situation of Sir Austin and Meredith in relation to women. I am indebted to her for the formulation of this point and for the stimulus I received from her views: her reading of the book and her conclusions, however, differ widely from mine.

(2) THE ADVENTURES OF HARRY RICHMOND

1 *Letters of Henry James*, ed. P. Lubbock (London, 1920), ii, 266.

2 Paul Goodman in *The Structure of Literature* (Chicago, 1954), p. 117, gives a valuable analysis of the necessity for the authorial presence to control mixed levels of seriousness.

3 'Is it not cowardly to lay all our sins at the door of the devil?' and 'The wishes we secretly nurse are the fathers of our future' (Maroon Notebook).

4 *The English Novel* (London, 1930), p. 89. Meredith's uneasiness about the propriety of explanation within an imaginative work is shown in a review he wrote for the *Fortnightly* in 1867 (n.s. i, 126). *La Maison Forestière* appealed powerfully to Meredith and he recounts the tale fully—a tale in which the image of the hunt is used as a poignant symbol of human longing and misunderstanding (as so often within Meredith's own work.) 'How Vittakab throws his son's body on the board spread for feasting, and speaks the "moral" in the presence of the marriage-guests . . . may be read in La Maison Forestière. It forms the climax explanatory, and will, I suppose, give greater satisfaction than if the emotions of the reader had not received assistance and directions.'

5 Quoted, Walter Phillips, *Dickens, Reade and Collins* (New York, 1962), p. 128. *The Letters of Charles Dickens*, ed. by his Sister-in-Law, ii, 249.

6 Quoted, Lionel Stevenson, *The Ordeal of George Meredith* (London, 1954), p. 76. Hereafter referred to as Stevenson. The original of this unpublished letter is at Yale.

7 For a full account of Meredith's problems with serialisation see R. A. Gettmann, 'Serialisation and *Evan Harrington*', *PMLA*, lxiv (1949), 963–75.

8 *George Meredith* (London, 1919), chs. i and vi. Viscountess Milner reports Meredith as telling her in old age that 'his father's sisters were the greatest ladies he had ever known.' 'As a child', he once told me, 'I was immensely tickled by the contrast between the tailor's shop and the princely family pedigree hanging in the back parlour'. 'A Talk about George Meredith', *National Review*, cxv (1940), 610.

9 Janet Duff Gordon was married in December 1860 to Henry Ross. The name Rose Jocelyne seems to be a play on Janet's married name. Poems addressed to Janet in 1859, as well as letters written at the time of the marriage, show how poignantly Meredith felt the fruitless situation in which he stood towards her: see *Letters*, i, 12, 17, 18, 20–2. *Evan Harrington* was written in 1859–60. (Janet Ilchester in *Harry Richmond* draws upon a more complex, less idealised conception of Janet Ross's personality.) Certain of the poems he wrote to Janet in 1859–60 explore imagery and moods soon to be dramatised in 'Modern Love'; compare the poem which begins:

> The waves are pressing up with force,
> Along the screaming shore;
> Like Phantom hosts of warrior horse,
> They charge beneath the roar. (*Letters*, i, 18)

and:

> In tragic hints here see what evermore
> Moves dark as yonder midnight ocean's force,
> Thundering like ramping hosts of warrior horse
> To throw that faint thin line upon the shore! ('Modern Love', L)

His feelings for Janet, as well as Mary's death in 1861, may have released in him the power and tragic consciousness of 'Modern Love'. *Evan Harrington* is the comic escape from experience, 'Modern Love' its ennobled confrontation.

10 R. Watson, '*Sandra Belloni*: the philosopher upon the sentimentalists', *ELH*, xxix (1957), 321–35, reads the philosopher's interjections as inartistic lecturing—but this is to miss the self-mocking burlesque.

11 The outline is published in full in 'Meredith's Autobiography and the Adventures of Harry Richmond', R. B. Hudson, *Nineteenth Century Fiction*, ix (1954).

12 Maxse, who was the model for that 'knight-errant of the nineteenth century', Nevil Beauchamp, is associated in Meredith's letters with the figure of Sir Harry Firebrand. (*Letters*, i, 220). This letter, dated 1870, was written in 1867 as a premonitory burlesque of what would happen to Maxse by 1870. See Stevenson, p. 162. The Aristophanes Portfolio includes a page noting a projected incident: Sir Harry defends a prisoner, 'it is the father of the gypsy girl'. The portfolio also includes two sides of pencilled notes describing the appearance, work, food, words, and names of Hampshire romany. In *Harry Richmond* these

hints take shape in the sub-plot of the gypsy girl, Kiomi. A full account of the fantasy of the 'knight-errant' in the form in which it was offered to H. G. Wells is given by Viscountess Milner, 'Talks with George Meredith', *National Review*, cxxxi (1948), 454–6.

13 Walter Houghton, *The Victorian Frame of Mind* (London, 1957), pp. 366–7.

14 First edition reads 'mightily'.

15 Dated 27 January 1851.

16 Coolidge, p. 49.

17 'I am amused from morning to night by Arthur's account of the "boys". It is as I suspected: he knows their characters consummately, I had the same faculty when I was young' (23 December 1862; *Letters*, i, 93). Meredith's account of this 'faculty' is ironic rather than admiring when he comes to write *Harry Richmond*.

18 The complete holograph is in the Altschul Collection, Yale University Library. MS Chapters xxx–xix were condensed at proof stage to become published Chapters xxx–xxxv. The whole manuscript was probably set up, as the compositors' marks indicate; the condensation took place before serialisation. The Altschul holograph therefore represents the work as Meredith envisaged it before commercial pressures obliged him to cut. It was serialised anonymously in the *Cornhill* to Meredith's chagrin (see *Letters*, i, 215). In the revised edition of 1886 Meredith cut four further chapters (see L. T. Hergenhan, 'Meredith's revisions of *Harry Richmond*', *Review of English Studies*, n.s. xiv (1963), 24). Meredith may have made the later cuts because he felt an imbalance in the structure of the book after the deletion of the chapters tracing the love of Ottilia and Harry. In the first edition he presents the process of reconciliation by which Janet and Harry at last come together. This tends to stress the Janet-Harry relationship beyond that of Ottilia and Harry. In the revised version the balance is righted at the expense of lessening the book's subtlety of analysis. Meredith's manuscript revisions almost always amplify the meaning; his revisions in proof and for later editions prune the form.

19 The heroine of Goethe's *Die Wahlverwandtschaften* is called Ottilia. Meredith said that the last of his formative reading was 'the noble Goethe, the most enduring' (*Letters*, ii, 577). He particularly admired *Die Wahlverwandtschaften* with its tersely economic and subtle analysis. *Wilhelm Meister* is importantly implicit in *Harry Richmond*. That novel uses the form of the *Bildungsroman*, and invokes German culture as an ideal within the work (expressed in diverse ways by the tutor Professor von Karsteg and the imaginative intellectual, Ottilia). The flight with the gypsies seems to be a conscious invocation of Goethe's novel. The mingling of fantasy and intellectual discussion parallels the conventions of the German rather than the English novel. *Harry Richmond* is concerned with the growth to intellectual and emotional maturity, 'the action of minds as well as of fortunes—of here and there men and women vitally animated by their brains at different periods of their lives' (Coolidge, p. 49).

Meredith's early methods absorbed elements from other European literatures. He admired both Stendhal and Flaubert at a time when they were little read in England. His 1858 review of *Madame Bovary*, in the *Westminster*

Review, was rare in its enthusiasm. A telling comment which he makes on the different moral effects of analysis and presentment has its bearing on his own work, and particularly on *Sandra Belloni*: 'If an adultery is to be treated at all . . . it should be laid bare—not tricked out in meretricious allurements: subjected to stern analysis—not made solely to present the passion, thereby to awake the sympathies of a vulgar prurience.' Meredith's fascination with analysis and his sense that it endangers emotion is seen again at this period in his comments on Stendhal's *L'Amour*: 'L'Amour ought not to be dissected and indeed can't be. For when we've killed it with this object, the spirit flies, and then where is L'Amour? Still I think de Stendhal very subtle and observant. He goes over ground that I know' (*Letters*, i, 57, 1861). Compare 'Modern Love' L, 1862: 'Then each applied to each that fatal knife, Deep questioning, which probes to endless dole.' (The translator of *Sandra Belloni*—first English edition, 1864; French translation, 1866—compares the novel to the work of Stendhal.)

20 *The Appropriate Form* (London, 1964), pp. 83–104.

21 The holograph of *Diana of the Crossways* (Morgan Library) elaborates this image, contrasting the reader's expectations of a holiday coach trip and the novelist's offering of 'a tumbled land of excavations'. 'Besides (& here lies the main point,) the mouth of a mine utters nothing but platitudes, let it be the very deepest of mines . . . unless we are willing to dismount, descend and explore . . .' (MS 1–2).

(3) BEAUCHAMP'S CAREER

1 See E. Clodd, 'George Meredith: some recollections', *Fortnightly Review*, n.s. dxi (1909), 27.

2 For discussion of the *Fortnightly Review* under the editorship of Meredith's close friend, Morley, see E. M. Everett, *The Party of Humanity: The Fortnightly Review and its Contributors*, Chapel Hill, 1939. Meredith himself acted briefly as editor in 1868. Norman Kelvin discusses the bearing of the *Fortnightly Review* and the ideals of Morley upon *Beauchamp's Career* in *A Troubled Eden*, Edinburgh and London, 1961, pp. 83–100. Kelvin reads *Beauchamp's Career* as a repudiation of the values of rationalism and of the demand that art should concern itself with 'questions of the day'. Meredith, he holds, uses and devalues these ideas within the work as an answer to Morley whose withdrawal of friendship had deeply wounded him.

3 Edith Wharton, *A Backward Glance* (New York, 1934), pp. 232–3.

4 See, for example, *Letters*, i, 165, 169–74, 176–9, 183–8.

5 See Ch. I, note 2, and Ch. II, note 12.

6 J. A. Hammerton quotes the anecdote on the authority of York Powell in *George Meredith: His Life and Art in Anecdote and Criticism*, rev. ed. (Edinburgh, 1911), p. 108.

7 '*Beauchamp's Career*: Meredith's acknowledgment of his debt to Carlyle', *Studies in Honor of John C. Hodges and Alwin Thayer* (Knoxville, 1961), p. 103.

8 cix, 539–472.

9 *Victorian Studies*, viii (1965), 309–27.

10 The green notebook in the Altschul collection was compiled while Meredith was working on *Beauchamp's Career*. It lists various anecdotes on 'Heroism—martial-domestic—Incidents'. The incidents range from Disraeli's wife suffering her finger shut in the carriage door to the Aborigines of Queensland eating men from among their own numbers rather than commit a breach of hospitality by eating the kangaroos in another tribe's territory! The hero of three of the episodes, Captain or Colonel Michell, is one of the off-stage 'heroes' in *Beauchamp's Career* whose courage in battle is never officially recognised (pp. 42, 94).

11 The scheme in the Maroon Notebook for the end of *Emilia in England* (*Sandra Belloni* was the title first in the revised edition) is both more melodramatic and more conclusive: 'She, first hears of poverty offers to try & make money. Wilfred pleads [poverty] his father's will to Emilia at a meeting. She goes to Mr Pole to entreat his aid and help to them (scene). Mr Pole, touched by her passion, tells her of his bankrupt state. Emilia writes to one of the Jews, offering to marry him at the immediate gift of £2000. The letter falls into the hands of Mr Powys—she receives money, makes appointment finds Mr Powys (scene) goes to Italy with him.'

12 (Oxford, 1963), p. 9.

13 Ramon Fernandez, 'The Message of Meredith' in *Messages* (London, 1927), pp. 155–90.

14 (London, 1890), pp. 120–32.

15 See his essay 'The Cynic of Society', *Pall Mall Gazette*, 28 March 1968.

16 'The Lesson of Balzac', in *The Future of the Novel*, ed. L. Edel (New York, 1956), p. 105.

17 *Granite and Rainbow* (London, 1958), p. 50. Originally printed in *The Times Literary Supplement*, 25 July 1918.

18 'But I am astonished that Mr X has separated my poetry from my prose. My thought unites itself spontaneously to prose and poetry, even as my flesh to my brain and my soul.' Quoted, Constantin Photiadès, *George Meredith: His Life, Genius and Teaching* (London, 1916), p. 9.

19 Professor Stevenson, in an article on 'Meredith and the Problem of Style in the Novel', in *Zeitschrift für Anglistik und Amerikanistik*, vi (1958), suggests that:

> 'He was determined to make each novel a work of literary art in the romantic tradition that expects the personality of the author to be an integral part of the total effect. He was equally determined to make it a subtle piece of analysis that would reward the respectful attention of intelligent readers. This double purpose is fulfilled by the interplay between the two types of personal statement—the poetic and the conversational.'

His view that Meredith's style is in part conversational is supported by the occasional articles which Meredith wrote for the *Pall Mall Gazette* in 1868. (see my 'Meredith's Contributions to the *Pall Mall Gazette*', *MLR*, lxv (1966).) But it is impossible to make a division between the conversational and the poetic statements in Meredith's novels. The occasional articles show that at its most conversational his writing is also at its most 'poetical'. In the novels Meredith controls and directs his habitual plethora of images, refining them into dramatically appropriate extensions of character or situation.

20 D. S. Austin gives a helpful collection of the discussions of metaphor in the novels: 'Meredith on the Nature of Metaphor', *University of Toronto Quarterly*, xxvii (1957), 96–101.
And compare:
'A brilliant saying arrests thought: a simple observation instigates it: an idea that fixes the mind to itself, cannot be of entire truth: one that leads it forth, altho' it be into the darkness, is the better guide. What we desire to hit is around us, not ahead, moving with us, around us.' 'A brilliant saying is a shot in the dark: a simple observation is the use of the eyes by daylight.' (Aristophanes Portfolio). The condensed version exemplifies the dangers of brilliance suggested in the first passage: the essence of the observation becomes vested for Meredith in the image.

(4) THE EGOIST

1 Memorial Edition, xxiii (London, 1910), p. 16.
2 Coolidge, p. 27. Letter to G. Bainton, 14 September 1887.
3 The situation in 'Modern Love' inverts that of *Othello*. In the modern world the husband's jealousy is grounded in the fact of his wife's guilt and violence is replaced by psychological cruelty. The situation of husband and wife is equally tragic. The poem echoes the play's imagery of light and the husband compares his situation to that of Othello:

I think she sleeps: it must be sleep, when low
Hangs that abandoned arm toward the floor;
The face turned with it. Now make fast the door.
Sleep on: it is your husband, not your foe!
The Poet's black stage-lion of wronged love,
Frights not our modern dames: well if he did. (xv)

4 This remark appears among a series of jottings in the Dramatic Dialogue Portfolio. '"None of your impudence", the young gentleman observed. "And none of your damned punctilio", said the man.' On the same page, recorded at the same time, is a remark that Meredith used in *Diana of the Crossways*, published six years before *One of Our Conquerors*: 'Old man looking at the cutting up of a "family" pig. "Ah could eat pig a solid hour": compare "Ah could eat hog a solid hower", *Diana*, viii; 98. The 'punctilio' incident may well have been the original germ of *One of Our Conquerors*.
5 *Saturday Review*, 27 March 1897.
6 Altschul Collection, Yale University Library. See my 'George Meredith and "The Satirist"', *Review of English Studies*, n.s. xv (1964), 283–95.
7 Aristophanes Portfolio. All the quotations are from the first page of notes on Aristophanes.
8 'Books which have Influenced Me', *Essays in the Art of Writing*, London, 1905.
9 n.s. lviii (1880), 287.
10 Willoughby imagines himself as the sun king (xiv; 161; xxxvii; 456).
11 *Aspects of the Novel* (London, 1927), pp. 87–8.
12 See R. D. Mayo, '*The Egoist* and the Willow Pattern', *ELH*, ix (1942), 71–8.

13 Dorothy van Ghent in *The English Novel: Form and Function* (New York, 1961), complains of this effect.

14 (Breslau, 1879). *Fortnightly Review*, n.s. v (1869), 419–53. For a more detailed discussion of Meredith's handling of his sources see my 'Meredith's Revisions of *The Tragic Comedians*', *Review of English Studies*, n.s. xiv (1963), 33–53.

(5) DIANA OF THE CROSSWAYS

1 *George Meredith* (London, 1956).

2 Meredith noted a similar incident among his MS notes (Dramatic Dialogue Portfolio): 'Some illustration of the Irony of Fortune=a writer in failing health has a Reversion of £20,000 coming to him from an old Relation, an imbecile lady of 75=the race between them: of the advantage this money wd. be to him She reaches 91 and dies one day after his burial.' Compare his letter to Arthur, 23 June 1881: 'I am to inherit from a relative, who is an old lady of 80 and more, and an imbecile, but extremely tenacious of her crazy hold of life; so that I see no holiday before me, and there are chances of my being outlasted' (*Letters*, i, 318).

3 The plot of Diana's novel is based on an incident recounted to her by Redworth—and shown to us as readers. Hence we can measure the extent of her distance from the actuality she exploits.

4 *Works*, ed. G. F. Maine (London, 1948), p. 915.

5 *English Criticism of the Novel 1865–1900* (Oxford, 1965), particularly pp. 61–70.

6 *The Letters of W. B. Yeats*, ed. A. Wade (London, 1954), p. 108.

7 In his correspondence with Lady Ulrica Duncombe, *Letters*, ii, 529–32, 542–3, he suggested that it would have been morally preferable for Diana's sexual virtue 'to have broken down in the accident of things' and so avoided her betrayal of Dacier. This is not presented as a meaningful possibility in the book itself.

(6) THE AMAZING MARRIAGE

1 I use the upper case N in Novelist to distinguish this figure from the author. In *One of Our Conquerors* (1891) 'the Dame' is Dame Nature: 'the Dame is up with her shrillest querulousness to inquire of her offspring for the distinct original motive of his conduct' (xix; 203). The manner here is very similar to that assigned to Dame Gossip: Dame Gossip is akin to Dame Nature in that she is a primitive force, not a personification of sophisticated social pressures.

2 Her description of her methods (iii; 27–8) contradicts the Novelist's description of them (xx; 209).

3 V. S. Pritchett takes the contrary view, *Books in General* (London, 1953), pp. 206–7.

4 *Letters of Henry James*, ed. P. Lubbock, ii, 455.

5 The Altschul Collection holds three fragments of early versions: the Nicholls version, 108 pp; the Cole version, 245 pp; Folder fragments, 3 pp. From internal evidence it would appear that the Nicholls version is the earlier, but portions of the Nicholls and Cole versions have been muddled together. In the

Cole MS is a second series of pages 248–310; these belong with the Nicholls version. Both Nicholls and Cole versions of the material I quote here are, therefore, actually included in the Cole manuscript. The scene described here runs from MS 259–87, Nicholls version; MS 270–300, Cole version.

6 The words are spoken by Gower Woodseer. His authority as a teacher (indicated by the elements of his name) is lightened but not impaired by his slightly buffoon role in the novel.

CONCLUSION

1 B. W. Matz quotes extracts from Meredith's early reports in 'George Meredith as Publisher's Reader', *Fortnightly Review*, n.s. lxxxvi (1909), 282–98. See also R. A. Gettmann, 'Meredith as Publisher's Reader', *Journal of English and Germanic Philology*, xlviii (1949), 45–56. The examples quoted in the text are from holograph notes in the Altschul Collection, Yale University Library, and date from the end of Meredith's career, 1889–94. His criteria do not change in the course of his career and these late examples are offered because they are less readily available for reference elsewhere.

2 I have written more fully about this aspect of *One of Our Conquerors* in an essay, '*One of Our Conquerors*: language and music' to be published in a collection edited by Ian Fletcher.

3 *The Letters of Henry James*, ed. P. Lubbock, i, 225.

4 *Aspects of the Novel*, p. 122.

5 Letter to Bainton, Coolidge, p. 27. Clodd, 'George Meredith: some recollections', *Fortnightly Review*, n.s. dxii (1909).

6 n.s. xi, 615.

7 These images are not peculiar to Meredith: they seem to have been current critical metaphors. Compare, for instance, *Blackwood's* reviews of *Adam Bede*: [we are] 'watching the operations of a skilful anatomist, as he lays bare the secrets of our quivering frame'; and 'We have here no morbid dwelling upon evil, nor yet an unreal optimism which dresses out life in hues of rose-colour.' *Blackwood's Magazine*, lxxxv (1859), 504.

8 *Ulysses* (London, 1937), pp. 187–8. See also Stanislaus Joyce, *My Brother's Keeper: James Joyce's Early Years*, ed. R. Ellmann (London, 1958), pp. 95, 205. Joyce's reservations about Meredith are expressed in the brief 1902 review of Walter Jerrold's *George Meredith*, where he says the novels have 'no value as epical art', though 'a distinct value as philosophical essays': *The Critical Writings of James Joyce*, ed. E. Mason and R. Ellmann (London, 1959), p. 88. See also D. Fanger, 'Joyce and Meredith: A Question of Influence and Tradition', *Modern Fiction Studies*, vi (1960), 125–30.

INDEX

Note. Meredith's published works are indexed alphabetically by title. Italic type indicates substantial discussion.